Grounded for LIFE?!

Grounded for LIFE?!

Stop blowing your fuse and start communicating with your teenager

Louise Felton Tracy, M.S.

Parenting Press, Inc.
Seattle, Washington

To you, Clif, and to our children,
Michael
Della
Teresa
Barbara
Matthew
Virginia
For the wonder of it all

———

First edition

Printed in the United States of America

Library of Congress Catalog Card Number 93-086232

ISBN 0-943990-95-5 Paperback
ISBN 0-943990-96-3 Library binding

Cover design by Cameron Mason
Cover illustration by Mits Katayama
Text design by Word Graphics, Inc.

Parenting Press, Inc.
P.O. Box 75267
Seattle, Washington 98125

Acknowledgments

Any person or work grows from the seeds planted and soil tilled by others. My deepest appreciation goes to family members, friends, mentors, and fellow workers who have contributed to my growth. I thank also those whose efforts have directly supported my work on this book. You and I know who you are, and you have made a difference!

Personal identification, however, belongs to three giants in the field of human growth who have, for years, directly and positively influenced my life and thousands of others. I extend my gratitude to:

- **Abraham H. Maslow,** for his research on successful people and his books that challenged me to embrace change and growth.
- **William Glasser,** for his Reality Therapy approach to counseling and his evidence concerning the impact one caring, reality-based person can have on another's life.
- **Thomas C. Gordon,** for the help he gave parents and the counseling world when he introduced his effective, global structure for communication skills through his Parent Effectiveness Training books and workshops.

To them we are all indebted.

Contents

Introduction

For years, parents have followed rules written by a society that says we are responsible for our children's health, safety, and success and for keeping those children well-behaved, happy, and popular. We should be able to cure pimples, pain, and crooked teeth. We ought to have the resources to supply our children with exciting vacations, brand-name jeans, and well-equipped bicycles.

No wonder we tend to believe that "parents know best," "obedience indicates learning," and if we could but do our job right, our children would be no problem to anyone. With such impossible standards, no wonder parents are discouraged!

Grounded for Life?! looks at the way parenting has been working and suggests a better way. It offers parents a child-rearing *process* that builds on communication, cooperative problem solving, and individual strengths. It teaches skills, presents life-changing options, and demonstrates relationship-building ways of involving adolescent children directly in their own growth. It promises on-the-job satisfaction for parents and everyday learning for children.

Grounded for Life?! is about making your job as a parent easier. The kind of parenting it promotes is neither authoritarian nor permissive, but instead recognizes the rights and responsibilities of both parents and adolescents. We refer to such parenting as *authoritative parenting*.

• Middle-School Age Children •

While the material in this book is applicable to the parent of any preteen or adolescent youngster, it directly addresses the parents of middle-school age children, ages 10 to 15 years. At this age our children still need us, and they know it. They're too young to drive and not old enough for the high-paying jobs that will bring them ready cash and freedom of time and movement.

The junior high and middle schools provide a relatively safe place for parents to begin the changes to authoritative parenting that this book teaches. While larger than the elementary schools, they are probably half the size of high schools. Supervision of students and dedication of staff to student and parent contact are still high, available, and personal. Generally, too, while middle-school age children may challenge adult wishes and authority, they do not actively deny them. This means we'll be getting our first practice in adolescent parenting on situations less risky to our children than those they will face in a few years.

• Today's Families •

While my husband's and my learning took place in a one-marriage, two-parent setting and this book has our family members as its main characters, the material is useful in all types of families. New or different living situations create unique challenges, but they do not determine a child's emotional health and behavior.

Growing research indicates an adolescent's behavior is more affected by the style of parenting under which he is reared and the quality of the parent-child relationship than by the type of family in which he resides. As a counselor working with hundreds of preteen and adolescent children and their parents and teachers in an educational setting, I've found that my family's learning transferred easily and effectively into all types of families.

• What Teens Want •

Extensive studies of adolescent children and the parenting styles under which they live indicate these children want parents who know how to be firm *and* how to be flexible. They want caring, involved parents who will help them balance their adolescent desires with life's responsibilities.

Authoritative parents are those who set clear standards for their adolescent children and expect mature behavior from them. These parents make rules, but are willing to discuss and possibly change them. They use commands and sanctions, but only when necessary.

These parents also recognize the rights of both parents and children and allow for an open communication that often involves verbal give-and-take. They routinely exhibit warmth and caring and encourage their adolescent's independence and individuality. Yet, they are rarely the first in the neighborhood to give a child adult freedom and privileges.

Research also indicates that parents who shift their style of parenting from authoritarian, indulgent, or neglectful patterns to an approach involving the elements listed above find major, positive changes occurring in their children's behavior within three to five months.

• Learning to Be Authoritative Parents •

Knowing the important elements of this effective style of parenting is the beginning of positive change—living it is the rest. In the chapters that follow, you'll see my engineer husband and me, the counselor wife, experience conflict with our six children and with each other. We'll argue for our positions, try different approaches, learn new skills, and grow with our kids through 23 years of continuous adolescence.

You'll be with us as we acknowledge that obedience is not synonymous with learning, help can be a four-letter word, and growth can be more important than success.

You'll see us vow to reject judgment, give up guilt, and stop solving our children's problems. Then, despite our best intentions, you'll see us get caught in old patterns again. You'll watch us buy ourselves time, learn to understand hidden emotions that have us trapped, and employ new ways of communicating. You'll see our children's real-life responses to our changing behavior.

Grounded for Life?! presents to you what I have found most usable from my years of counseling training, professional experience, and our ever-changing home life. It offers you a rock-solid foundation of communication built on love that will benefit you and your children every day of your lives.

1

Challenging Children, Challenged Parents

New Belief: *It doesn't make sense to use again and again an approach that has proven itself ineffective, yet expect each time it will produce good results.*

• The Middle-School Years •

Our children forget their homework, choose the "wrong friends," talk back, overeat, undereat, and get poor grades. They avoid chores, vegetables, and all the clothes we like. They're irrational, irreverent, stubborn, and shy.

We get calls from their teachers. Our children are disruptive in class or uncooperative on school grounds. They suffer from lack of motivation, poor self-esteem, or bad study habits. They talk too much and are overly aggressive and easily distracted.

Yesterday, the bigger problems were in our high schools. Today, they're in our middle schools. Statistics tell us most children will have experimented with alcohol and tobacco by the end of eighth grade. Fifteen percent will have experimented with other drugs. Many will be sexually active and a few will have contracted a sexually transmitted disease, or had a baby or an abortion.

Children with a record of past behavior problems, and those with none, will be caught lying to a responsible adult, cutting school, using four-letter words, smoking, or cheating. Each year some with stolen goods or illegal substances in their possession will be arrested and spend time in juvenile hall.

We know our youngsters are growing up too fast. We talk to teachers, establish study hours, and tighten our rules. We listen to their phone calls. We check and double-check. Consistency and firm discipline become our bywords. Family discussions that begin with justifiable concerns end in arguments, accusations, and punishment.

Life moves from crisis to crisis; we deliver ultimatums and our children fight them. We insist they stop, listen, and obey, but in the process we become their enemies.

Most approaches to child rearing get children to respond to parental wishes some of the time. It doesn't follow, however, that these children agree with us in principle or continue in the same path when out of our sight.

Regardless of our love and protection, wisdom and effort, our children will move outside our control.

Most of us living with a preteen or adolescent youngster function with serious doubts about our child-rearing methods. We worry because the results come with pain and force, rather than cooperation. We hate ourselves for the words we use, the anger we experience, and the behavior we model. Later, when we hear our young adult remember in great detail a punishment, but unable to recall the behavior that caused it, we know there has to be a better way.

• Changing Times, Challenging Children •

Our family had one particularly difficult year. My husband Clif was experiencing health problems. Our children were at four different school levels and our bright, oldest son Mike, who we'd pressured and punished for years trying to change his marginal academic performance, was now failing in his first semester of college. Our high-school daughter Della, whose safety and health had been our number one priority since her birth, was skipping the back exercises her doctor had ordered, eating junk food, smoking, and we suspected, hitchhiking. Every morning we had a confrontation, often leaving her in tears and me feeling guilty.

The middle ones, Teresa and Barbara, offered us morning hassles, sibling arguments, and a budding adolescence too full of social activities for our comfort. The younger two, Matt and Ginny, complained of my inability to participate in their lives as much as they wished, and resented the changes forced upon them following my necessary return to full-time work after Clif's illness.

• The Signs of Conflict •

As parents, we all know we have problems. Children roll their eyes at our wisdom and ignore our warnings. They give us minimum information and ridicule our worries. They use their intelligence and energy to get parental permission to do as they wish, and if that fails, then that same energy is applied to doing it without parental knowledge. Panic touches our hearts and we wonder if we're losing our children.

We threaten, take away, and ground. We yell, order, and demand. Sometimes we slap. We try harder, pray more, and worry constantly. We hate our behavior as well as theirs and wonder how all this began.

When our oldest child questioned our authoritarian approach, we jokingly replied that our home wasn't run as a democracy but as a benevolent dictatorship. We shouldn't have been surprised when no one laughed. Obedience was costly and changing attitudes was difficult.

Any complacency we'd ever experienced was gone. Just keeping the house reasonably clean and the family basically functioning required hours of our attention and made us angry. Nightly, Clif and I went to sleep with the words of battle ringing in our ears and our hearts hurting.

• Judgment, the Stepping Stone into Conflict •

For several months I had been taking classes to prepare myself to move from a community agency into a public-school counseling position. The thought of being a middle-school counselor both challenged and troubled me. If I knew so much, why weren't all our good-hearted intentions and conscientious efforts working at home?

One day I attended a communications class and found the word *judgment* written in large letters on the blackboard. At the end of the class, the instructor touched the word and asked us to observe ourselves and our interactions with family members for the next few days. "Make a note each time you make a judgmental comment to someone," he said. "And remember, each time you give your opinion, express a belief, or make a suggestion, you're involved in judging."

Everything I said needed writing down. With parental helpfulness, I *questioned* their wisdom and *expressed* mine: "Are you sure you want to take shop?" "Pink isn't your color, wear the white one." "I wouldn't lend it to him if I were you—he's not responsible." Hair, clothes, schoolwork, or the day's plans—if the child didn't ask for my wisdom, I volunteered it.

My opinions were clear as I *criticized* and *praised*: "Your paper looks too messy." "That skirt is too short." "Great work—see what you can do if you try?"

Judgment was there as I *ordered, directed,* and *advised*: "It's cold, wear a sweater." "So you're late, brush your teeth anyway." "Don't rush, you'll break something."

Nothing missed my attention. In my attempts to *comfort* and *motivate,* I judged: "It's just one game. No big deal. You'll do better next time." "Copy it over, you hurried too much."

My involvement was extensive. I was a busy mother and things had to be settled, and settled fast. I knew what was best for our children and I was making it happen. Wasn't I only doing what any good parent does? I thought so, until my experience in the communications class made me stop and think again.

• Wanted: A Listener •

One morning Della came out alternately pulling her sweater down and bunching it up. "Do you like this on me?" she asked.

Holding back the words forming in my mind, I murmured, "Hmmm, sounds like you don't. What's the matter?"

"Oh," she bubbled forth, "it makes me look so long and skinny, look how it clings to me...." On she rambled, telling me of her concerns with the color, shape, and material. Then suddenly, she smiled casually, and said, "Oh, well, I'll wear it anyway. What's one day of looking creepy?"

I couldn't believe it! She didn't want my opinion. All she wanted was a listener. No wonder we had all those morning arguments, when I sat in judgment.

• Teen Choices, Parent Discomfort •

Still, if that were so, why did I have this terribly uncomfortable feeling inside of me? Why did I feel, as she walked out the door, that I should call her back, tell her the sweater was too long and clingy, and even though her best friend had given it to her, she shouldn't wear it—ever!

Even if she could handle how she looked, I couldn't. I didn't want our child looking creepy and unattractive and both of us getting a D grade for her appearance. Yes, I was grading *myself* on her appearance, achievements, health, and popularity. I stopped, dumbfounded.

That night as Clif and I talked about the situation, we realized we'd operated for years with the belief that it was our job to know what was right and good for our children, follow through on it, and to the best of our ability, keep them from experiencing failure, embarrassment, ill health, pain, and every other negative thing life inevitably serves up.

An impossible goal, of course, but many of us believe in it. Understandably so, considering the bombardment of information parents receive from the experts about the physical, social, and emotional needs of children that must be met by parental love and care. When we add to that the media's tantalizing image of what makes the American child's life worth living, the underlying message we get is clear: *Parents* are the key to their children's successes.

The major problem with this belief is that it doesn't allow children the opportunity for the emotional growth they must have if they are to survive in their own world successfully. Children deserve the right to make their own mistakes and learn from them.

• Life-Given Circumstances •

In general, you may agree that children should take more responsibility for their own lives, but what if a child has a birth injury, a learning disability, or has had to change schools every year? What if you're on welfare, there's been a divorce, a death, or a disabling accident in your family? What if you don't speak English? What if your child was adopted and you know her prenatal care was inadequate? Are you not then responsible?

Each parent's list is filled with things that affect their children through no fault of their own. Clif and I asked ourselves: "Would this be happening if I'd not gone to work full time, we'd had fewer children, she weren't caught in the middle, there'd been no allergies or hearing loss problems in our family?"

We can't change many of these life-given circumstances, but we do feel anxious about and responsible for them. Gradually, the negative effect we believe the situation is having on a particular child seems so great that we work doubly hard to compensate.

However, with most of us, trying harder doesn't get us the results we want. We need to accept the fact that misfortunes exist and blaming them for a child's poor behavior or lack of success is unproductive and potentially makes the circumstance more of a handicap.

In our family, all our supervision and effort couldn't make Mike want to do his schoolwork or prevent Della from skipping her exercises and putting on more makeup once she was out of our house. We couldn't keep the younger children from expertly forging our name on a school excuse or attending unsupervised parties. In fact, once out of a parent's presence none of our children can be prevented from running with the wrong crowd, cutting school, failing, drinking, smoking, driving recklessly, or having sex!

We know a rebellious child can: (1) skillfully circumvent our supervision, (2) decide to openly defy us, risk our anger, and take the consequences, or (3) minimally cooperate until age or graduation frees him to do anything he wishes without our consent or involvement.

With privileges and rewards, disapproval and punishments, we might get a specific behavior change for a period of time, but it doesn't mean the young person has accepted our standards as her own or even agrees with us about their importance.

• Eighteen Years of Dependency? •

Yes, with our national commitment to compulsory education and effective child-labor laws, parenthood has evolved into 18 years of parental responsibility, but is this appropriate? We know our children are maturing faster. The onset of puberty in boys and girls has dropped approximately two years since the early 1900s, but their greatest change is not physical.

Consider the information and instruction our preteen children receive today from the media and their community about sex, violence, drugs, and crime. The sophistication of experiences, clothes, and language they bring to middle school are years beyond that of their parents, and even more so of their grandparents, at the same age. Yet, when researchers compare the first intelligence tests given in 1916 with those given in this decade, our children have not changed intellectually.

Since their cultural environment has changed so dramatically, we as parents need to adjust our parenting to meet the reality of their lives. Middle-school age children deserve the opportunity to become as emotionally mature as they are physically and socially mature.

After high school, children's choices are unlimited and the consequences costly. Already our older two often seemed oblivious to the high price they might pay in health, safety, or opportunities for a moment of fun, excitement, or peer approval.

Clif and I asked ourselves if we were doing them a grave injustice by not allowing them the serious decision-making practice they needed at home to prepare themselves for their adult lives. Were we teaching our children to think or to argue? To be responsible or simply to obey?

Nothing was simple. Even the smallest situation came loaded with potential problems. Yet we were the only ones who seemed to worry about their choice of friends, study habits, and what the neighbors thought. So much worry for us and so little satisfaction—all with the idea of keeping our children safe, healthy, happy, well-behaved, successful, smart, pretty, popular.

We shook our heads. "There has to be a better way. It's her back, his lungs, and their skin complexions. It's her reputation, his college opportunity, his yard job and relationship with the neighbor. We talk ourselves hoarse and still they can do what they want, their way, if they so decide. Our parenting is not working," we agreed. "Let's change it!"

Just because that's the way it's always been, doesn't mean that's the way it has to be.

Challenging Children,
Challenged Parents

• Steps to Change •

Consider your situation. Do you lack confidence in your child-rearing approach? Do you and your child's interactions often end with one of you unhappy? If so, *prepare* yourself for change.

Adopt new beliefs. Parents are not responsible for everything that happens to their teenagers. Teens need daily opportunities to think about problems, make decisions, and make mistakes.

Listen to yourself talk. Be aware of your judgmental statements. They invite arguments and limit your child's ability to solve problems.

Become a listener on minor concerns. Show your attention with "hmmm," "oh," "I guess," followed by a few brief words recognizing the problem. Watch your child resolve a concern without your input.

Be patient with yourself. Allow yourself growing time. For years, you've protected your child from embarrassment, inconvenience, and unhappiness. Change *is* difficult.

Believe in change. Every worthwhile improvement begins with one person's dissatisfaction, followed by a risk-taking step.

2

Begin by Changing Yourself

New Belief: *Growth, confidence, and self-esteem come from the inside out, not vice versa.*

• Who Owns the Problem? •

While Clif and I were willing to admit that we were overly involved in the day-to-day management of our children's lives, we had to wonder if we could really change. We'd been in charge for 18 years and things could have been a lot worse. Fortunately, our children furnished us with new evidence daily that our old parenting style simply wasn't producing the responsible children we wanted and the relationships we all needed.

One school morning, our oldest daughter Della and her 13-year-old sister Teresa were already running late when they began talking about rebraiding Della's hair. I glanced at the clock and my response was automatic: "You don't have time. Your hair looks fine. You'll miss your bus. Hurry up . . . and don't forget your lunch!"

Oh, no. There I was worrying about getting Della out the door, so *she* wouldn't miss *her* bus, so *she* wouldn't be late and have to serve *her* detention. This was their business, it didn't have to affect me.

After they left, I made a list of the things our youngsters were doing that caused me concern and ended with me being in a position of judging their behavior and trying to get the problem resolved. Then I asked myself three key questions:

- Who do the results of this situation directly affect in the long run?
- Who should be thinking about how to solve the problem?
- Who has the power to make the solution succeed?

Some items I marked with a child's name, some with mine. It was a fine starting point. Obviously, not all the problems could be handled by just one person, but I decided to begin with situations clearly belonging to our children.

As I reviewed the situations in the light of the three questions, I realized the problems I'd marked with a youngster's name had been around for a while. There were school and neighborhood problems, sibling and peer squabbles, lost belongings, forgotten lunches, and missed dental appointments. Apparently working at resolving our children's problems was a major way we related to our children.

• Give Children Power Over Themselves •

One day as I was leaving for work, 11-year-old Barbara stopped me in tears. "My social studies report! I forgot it was due today and it has to be copied. What am I going to do? It's worth half my grade for the term and it's due first period!"

Her anguish was genuine. She was an outstanding student, and this could spoil a two-year stretch of terrific grades. Ideas flooded my mind. But, no! Give her attention, give her concern, but no solutions, no answers, I reminded myself.

"Oh, honey, what a bad spot, and you've worked so hard on your report, too. All that time in the library, the pictures . . ." I took a deep breath, reached for her hand and held on tight. "I don't know what to suggest. I'm so sorry, I have an early meeting and I have to go." I gave her a heartfelt hug, smoothed her hair from her face, and turned to leave. Then it popped out, "You're smart. I'll bet you can think of something."

Whew! I'd mothered, but I'd not solved the problem for her. I felt great. "I don't know"— what wonderful words. "I don't know what kind of dress you should wear; if your gym clothes will pass as washed; whether you should play on your hurt ankle or not." Then, how easy it was to add, "What do you think? What are your ideas on it? How have you considered handling it?"

Perhaps you have a child with braces who is being too casual about teeth brushing and is seemingly unconcerned by the dentist's warning of permanent stains.

Hear in your head the judgmental warnings you're issuing— interrupt yourself right in the middle of your sentence and openly acknowledge your over-involvement in what doesn't directly affect you.

Say out loud, "Listen to me going on. You'd think your teeth were in my mouth. You don't need me telling you when and how to brush your teeth. You know when they need brushing better than I do, and from now on, I'll be leaving their care in your hands. Your teeth are yours, and you'll do what is best for them, I'm sure."

What if she doesn't brush and her teeth are permanently stained? Isn't it better your daughter learn on teeth that her body is her responsibility than while drinking and driving a car, diving into a shallow lake, or riding a motorcycle recklessly? These, and any of a hundred other incidents, cripple and kill adolescents each year. Teeth may be one of the less costly places our children have to learn about the ways their bodies respond to their care.

• Learn to Listen •

I've modeled for you the way I would like to have handled the teeth situation on our family's first case of braces, and didn't. *We begin by hearing ourselves say the wrong thing,* and then, since our children always give us second chances, we get better at saying the right thing. By the third time, we get great!

In one of my classes, we talked about Carl Rogers, a noted counselor, and how he listened to his clients. We watched him in action on video, and I was impressed with the way he avoided any response that placed his judgment, personality, or feelings onto his client.

Professionally, he was a master listener who had many ways

of letting the person he was with know he was there to hear with his heart, body, and mind. There was the quiet room, his attentive body position, facial expressions of interest, and his intense, focused eye contact. Occasionally, there was a nod of his head, a slight, warm smile of awareness, an "oh," "ah," or "hmmm," but never an interruption with advice, suggestions, warnings, or those "uplifting" phrases we all have on the tip of our tongues for our children.

Could I use these same skills when any of our children met me at the end of the day, upset or angry, complaining or worried?

Could I do what I was already doing with adult clients in their times of stress or distress? First, I'd listen to what my children said with my complete attention, then summarize in my own words what they said, and, last, I'd acknowledge their feelings, expressed or shown. Then I'd wait for the youngster to confirm my understanding, add more information to the subject if he wished, or correct me if I were wrong in what I'd understood or noted.

Maybe with this approach I could avoid those judgmental statements that popped out of my mouth and seemed to lead me so quickly into arguments and solving their problems.

The first step to change is recognizing what to change.

• Use New Knowledge •

There had been a night meeting and I was late getting home. Ginny, who was then in the sixth grade, looked up from her homework at the dining room table and said scathingly, "Mom, why'd you have so many kids when you're never home with us?"

"Okay." (Deep breath now) "Take it easy. You're tired, but all you have to do is hear her, not defend your whole life," I thought to myself.

"You're right, I am gone a lot, and twice this week at night," I said, as my hand touched her shoulder. I sat down near her. "I'm here now. Let's talk."

"No! You're too tired, go on to bed. Besides," she added, picking up her pencil and focusing on her papers, "it's not important."

Oh, how easy it would be to accept her words at face value, but would I do that with a youngster at school?

I inched my chair closer to hers and put both my hands on her arm. "It's hard, isn't it? Even when I'm here, there are always the emergencies, the older ones, the other ones, and your dad. We're a big family and with me working I guess it could seem I don't have time for you. That's not the way I want it to be."

She lifted her face, and the tears that had collected in her eyes overflowed. "Oh, Mom, it's awful! You won't believe what happened. Can we go to your bedroom?"

She'd heard at lunch that one of her friends had polled everyone in their group on whether or not she should include Ginny in an overnight pool-and-slumber party she was having the next weekend. The no's had won.

Ginny's face held the grief of a child who has just seen her dog hit by a car. "What am I going to do? I thought they were my friends. How can I go to school and talk to them?"

———

With our first child I'd have believed it was my responsibility as a parent to help her search for the truth in the situation. I would have asked: Was she sure her informer was honest and accurate? Were the girls just teasing and she taking it too seriously? How about her own behavior? What could she have done to make her friends all vote against her?

Note the thoughts I'd have brought into this situation and the judgmental statements I would have made to our child about her perceptions and actions.

I could tell you in detail of our failures and the situations we'd like to have handled differently, but modeling good behavior for you is better than modeling bad. Just as with children and their growth, Clif's and mine came in steps. Even though we knew better, we often continued to do things in the old way. This time I handled Ginny differently.

———

I held her as she sobbed and listened as she talked of not knowing who had voted against her and who had not. As she shared the depths of her grief, my eyes filled with tears, but when she asked, "What can I do?" I shook my head. "I don't know, but since you've been living with this all day, something must have come to your mind."

A smile touched her lips as she nodded. "I could go to school tomorrow, act like I always do, smile at them, be friendly, but not hang around them. If someone talks to me, I could mention my plans to be out of town next weekend visiting my sister at college. Then it would seem like I didn't expect an invitation. I could leave Friday after school. It would be okay, wouldn't it, Mom?" Her smile was real now.

Later she added, "It's going to be all right, but they're not my friends anymore. I'll make new ones."

How our children surprise us once we allow them to solve their own problems.

• Does Help Really Help? •

For three years in a row, the seventh-grade students at the middle school where I counseled identified problems with their peers as their number-one school concern. Unfortunately, as parents, teachers, and school counselors, we often think we understand these situations and believe we can resolve them with our reassurance, advice, and action. Often this doesn't work. Such approaches miss the heart of the matter and are seldom more than a Band-Aid for the pains that come to our attention.

———

Late one night I heard our 13-year-old Teresa sobbing in the bathroom. "Oh, Mom," she said, as I put my arms around her, "you don't know what it's like being in eighth grade and having no one to eat with at lunchtime!"

"No, I don't know," I whispered. "But I've never heard you cry like this before. It must be terrible."

"It is. I don't belong to any group. I've tried everything to look busy: working in the cafeteria, being an office aide, studying in the library. It never ends, every night I have to think about tomorrow."

———

Did my heart hurt for this daughter? You know it did, but not as it would have a few weeks earlier.

For years, we'd known this youngster was quieter than our

others, less aggressive and social. Someone else borrowed the vanilla from the neighbor, took the cookies to the new family moving in, or called for her orthodontist appointments. Her siblings included her in their social activities with their peers. I called her counselor when schedule changes were needed. I'd even made her last birthday party a surprise one.

Recently, I'd read the helpful book *Liberated Parents, Liberated Children* by Adele Faber and Elaine Mazlish, and been struck by a remarkable statement they attributed to Dr. Haim Ginott.

Dr. Ginott suggested that to change behavior in a child, you treat your child as if she were already what you want her to become.

I realized that for years I'd been treating this daughter as if she were shy, and sending, with my every action, a confirming statement about her inability to cope with her own social needs. Sadly, I remembered my enthusiastic push for clubs and the suggestions I made regarding her friendliness with the new children at school.

I had already begun trying to live Dr. Ginott's profound statement in my every contact with Teresa. My guideline was simple: Just respond to her each time as I would to her verbal, popular, socially confident older sister.

Without consciously understanding it, could our daughter have realized I was no longer so judgmental about her behavior, so anxious for her social growth, so fearful for her unhappiness? I was trying to change the way I handled the children's concerns and watching my words with everyone. Did she now know I could handle her pain?

———

That night as we talked, I listened with my heart, not my mind. I heard her words and her feelings, and put them in my own words. "It's so lonely, such an everyday, ongoing thing."

In the stress of the moment, if I couldn't rephrase it, I just repeated her words. "It's so bad you just want to get away, leave, not have to think about friends and lunchtime ever again."

She herself had just said these words, but now she looked at me and nodded her head at my understanding. "On the way to school sometimes I think about getting sick, getting some disease that will keep me home."

"Oh, honey." It was all I could say as I held her close. We were sitting on the bath mat now, and I rocked her gently, smoothed her hair, and listened as she talked and cried over her years of pretending and covering up. "How long this has been going on, and you've just kept carrying it inside you, trying to solve it." Finally the tension eased from her face and voice, and I could feel her body relax.

Knowing now she could hear, I told her what I wished for her, even if it was unrealistic: "I wish that I could sprinkle you with star dust and all of this would go away, but that's not the way problems are resolved, is it?"

She shook her head, and I continued: "You've tried so hard, everything and more than I could suggest. Maybe there's no answer right now. Maybe this is your year to be lonely, to pull into yourself, think about you, about what you like to do, and who you are."

She talked again about school, her efforts there, and the social activities everywhere she'd forced upon herself. Then suddenly, her voice strong and her eyes shining, she declared, "I'll keep baby-sitting at church, but no more Camp Fire Girls!"

I smiled and nodded. "You know what is right for you. You've had friends before," and I named some. "You listen, keep secrets, and stay loyal. Everyone in the family goes to you with their hurts and problems. You know how to make friends, and when you're ready, you'll have them again. Good ones."

• Accepting Differences Fosters Self-Esteem •

Several days later, quite unexpectedly, Teresa said, "You know that area in back of the garage, the catchall place? Could I clean it out, dig it up, maybe get some plants, and put in a brick walk?"

A month ago, my approval would have been instant. I would have been filled with ideas and we would have made a quick trip to the local nursery and hardware stores. I'd have wanted to be encouraging and helpful. Now? No. If this were our eager, bubbling, full-of-ideas, older daughter, I'd be cautious and find out what she had in mind before committing even my enthusiasm to a project. I decided to try this approach with Teresa, so that I wouldn't seem to be pushing her.

"The area does need improvement," I conceded, then I stopped. Here I was talking with my back to her and my eyes on the meat I was browning. "Wait, let me finish this and we'll sit down. I'm interested in what made you think of this."

Our usually quiet daughter spent the next 10 minutes telling me how good she was with plants, that she could always revive Barbara's dead ones, and that even her cuttings lived. She said she'd found a book about California landscaping in the school library and she'd been thinking about a bench she and her younger brother Matt might make for under one of the trees. Finally, she asked, "How much money do you think I could spend on plants and stuff?"

I summarized with interest what she'd said and then, as if this idea were coming from her older sister, I said, "Sounds fine, but we'll have to talk to your dad."

Clif responded with practical restraint. "Sketch it out and give me some ideas on paper. We'll figure the cost, and go from there."

Did this youngster suddenly become an outgoing social butterfly? Is she one now? No, but she's a talented, many-faceted, happy adult with her own family, work, and good friends. During her high school years she became interested in sewing, quilting, and designing clothes. She found a wooden trunk on a trash heap and a love for refinishing and owning old furniture was born.

If you give your children the power to solve their own problems, they will learn effective ways to do so with their own resources.

Teresa's talents were not mine, nor anyone else's in the family. We couldn't help her with her interests, so she found people who could. She was an eager learner; she had ideas and time. People in hardware and fabric stores, hobby shops, and antique stores appreciated her interest and efforts, and recognized her eye for color and design, and her commitment to detail.

Her interests were not group-oriented, competitive, or social, yet daily they shaped her personality, confirmed her strength, and built her confidence.

Growth, confidence, and self-esteem all truly come from the inside out, not vice versa. In the next chapter, you'll see Clif and me begin our own steps towards honoring each other's individuality as well as our children's.

Begin by Changing Yourself

• Steps to Change •

Decide who owns the problem. Make a list of the things your teen does that concern you. Identify the problems for which he or she *should* be responsible.

Acknowledge the child's ownership. Pick a definite problem and plan to relinquish it lovingly. Parents can't fix problems they don't own.

Make your listening count. Really listen to what your teen is saying. Make eye contact. Don't interrupt. Put in your own words the problem he presents. Acknowledge his feelings.

Upgrade your opinion of your child. Avoid offering help, advice, solutions, generalizations, probing questions, and judgments.

Communicate positive feelings. Treat your child as if she is already the person you want her to become. Verbalize your confidence in your kid's ability to manage a situation.

Recognize that changing behavior requires practice. Don't panic when you flip back into your old "responsible-parent" behavior, fears, and voice. Acknowledge your over-involvement and your desire to change. Begin again.

3

Divide and Communicate

New Belief: *Children learn important life skills when they deal with their parents as individuals with different talents, priorities, limitations, and feelings.*

• Each Parent Is Unique •

The problems with children during their preteen and adolescent years often escalate into arguments between parents. Our children are now older and smarter, and the issues they bring to our lives are bigger. Their motivation to win is greater. They also know each adult's values, beliefs, strengths, and weaknesses, and how he or she will react to a well-placed plea or statement.

The united-parent stance that may have worked while our youngsters were small now seems to be translating into united when parents agree and each parent arguing for the voice of authority when we don't. Unfortunately, this may lead, in the stress of a disagreement, to the "voice of authority" coming out of one parent or the other's childhood experiences, health, fatigue, fears, or prejudices rather than a reasonable view of the problem.

For single parents, the home situation may be different from Clif's and mine, but the material in this chapter is still relevant. You may find your adolescent using the same divide-and-conquer technique on relationships between you and other adult figures in your life: grandparents, aunts and uncles, older siblings, special friends or companions, or the out-of-the-home parent.

As a counselor-parent, I tended to see things in shades of gray, understood our youngsters' desires for independence and favor with their peers, and felt Clif often had unrealistic expectations for their performance. He, on the other hand, was a highly organized test engineer in the space industry. He was trained in making instant decisions and having them followed. He saw things in black and white and flinched at the things I didn't see or could simply ignore.

He thought about utility bills. I focused on the children's fears. He wanted items where they belonged, I wanted them nearby. He was concerned that his tools be used correctly and returned to the garage. I was delighted to have our son positively occupied and saw the tools more as learning objects than prized possessions.

We couldn't even imagine all the situations we found ourselves facing, much less have the time to negotiate a united position prior to our involvement with a child. Even when our intentions were good, the results weren't. Both of us were somehow becoming more and more openly critical of the way the other was handling a child or situation.

• Conflicting Views •

Take the tools, as Clif did the day he found them scattered in our driveway. Matt, the child user, wasn't home, so Clif expressed his anger to me. I listened and with a Solomon-like wisdom explained how hard our son had worked on the item he was making for his fort and of his unexpected invitation to go with a neighbor into town.

These were extenuating circumstances from my viewpoint. Clif relaxed and I agreed to talk again with Matt about *his father's* wishes.

Another day dawned and Clif needed his tools. This time he found them rusting in the back yard. All his smoldering anger surfaced. He yelled, grabbed our son from his bike, and marched him into the house, "How dare you treat my tools like that? Take off your baseball uniform and get some rags for cleaning. Now!"

"But, Dad, I can't! It's a game, not just practice."

Note the arrow our son has just shot into *my* values, fears, and ego. He'll lose face with his teammates. What will this do to his confidence, his desire to play ball, stay in Little League? Is the discipline too harsh? What will the coach and other parents think about our son, about us?

I touched Clif's shoulder, and the scenario began. "Honey, the game's against West Valley. He can't miss that. You'd be punishing the team, not just him. Besides, I should have reminded him about the tools. It was late and I knew it might rain."

See how good intentions, extenuating circumstances, and conflicting views can change the focus? Suddenly, Clif's in a no-win situation—the one injured but without a culprit. "Then why didn't you remind him?" he snarled at me. Just as quickly, I snapped back, "Because I can't remember everything with six kids!" And off we went.

• One-Parent Ownership of a Problem •

With every passing day, Clif and I were in conflict. Often it seemed our children were tearing us apart. Then one night I walked in to hear our 16-year-old Della telling her father he was the only man in the world who would distrust his daughter so much he'd keep track of where she went by checking the car mileage. "And then to say I can't use the car Saturday just because I drove some friends home from play practice isn't fair!"

"Yes," Clif said, "but you didn't mention all the miles on the freeway and in the mountains when you asked for the car. That's thirty miles on a rainy night instead of six!"

"But you promised! My friends give me rides all the time. They're counting on me. If I let them down, how can I ever ask them to drive me anywhere again?"

Right then, her arrow hit the one spot guaranteed to get me on her side. All six children knew we depended heavily on ride sharing. Still, this time I hesitated, and in that instant, there came a major shift in our family's approach to problem solving.

"No!" Clif said. "Car pooling and ride sharing are between you and your mother. The car, its care, and your use of it are between you and me."

Serendipity. Cars were his responsibility. He handled their maintenance, repairs, and replacement. He took care of out-of-gas and car-won't-start calls. He dealt with insurance, completed accident reports, and really cared about the thousand and one things car usage entails.

I withdrew and their discussion ended quickly. Clif knew what was right for him, and our daughter understood he'd not be swayed by the circumstances that had so touched me.

When she came to me later in tears, pleading her loss of credibility with her friends, reminding me of her good grades, and asking that I intercede, I wasn't surprised. Often I did, but this time my vision was broader. Did the results of this situation directly affect me? Did Clif and I, with our dramatically different personalities, have to somehow reach mutual agreement on every problem we had with our children? No!

I didn't have to decide whether Clif was right or wrong, or defend his or our daughter's actions. This was between them. What I could do was *actively listen* to her anger as she exploded over his decision, and not try to answer her words with reason and common sense.

However, when she asked me again to talk to her father, I was able to say with conviction, "I can't do it. This problem is between you and your dad; you'll have to talk to him yourself."

Looking back, it seems strange that one-parent ownership of problems was such a revelation to Clif and me.

• Dividing the Problem Areas •

What would happen if Clif and I openly gave the authority and the responsibility for certain family situations to one or the other of us? We each argued now for the right to have the deciding voice in sensitive situations. At any given time, one of us was positive he or she could make a better decision than the other, based on his or her wisdom, experience, and personality.

If your situation is one where problems cannot be divided between two cooperating adults, then try dividing some of them with your adolescent. Adolescents are of an age and temperament to want to have final authority and responsibility for as many areas of their lives as possible. Begin on some problems that the adolescent wants to see resolved effectively.

There is much evidence to indicate that our children respond well to new responsibilities when assuming them does not involve parental punishment, emotional outbursts of anger and blame, or the use of external rewards.

Identify the problems. To identify problems that might benefit from such division, consider major problem areas and ask yourself:

- What do I really want my child to gain, learn, or experience from this situation?
- When does this learning have to happen?
- How does it have to happen?
- Does it have to happen in a certain way?

———

A widow with a seventh-grade son was deeply distressed over her son's ongoing careless use of his father's excellent hand tools. She knew the tools would mean a lot to him when he was older and she wanted them kept in good condition for the future.

After she responded to the above questions, she realized that her real desire was that these tools give her son a sense of closeness with his father and help him understand his father's personality, skills, and dedication to his work. "Maybe using the tools now with his friends is more important for that than having the tools later. And if some get lost or rusted . . ." Suddenly she smiled, "Well, the problems really directly affect only him!"

This mother told me later that, after several weeks, her son suddenly placed a clipboard and a box near his father's tools. He had decided to have his friends sign their names and leave something like a watch or wallet with him when they borrowed a tool. "Then maybe I won't always be asking them to bring back Dad's things," he said.

Clif and I started with some obvious issues for us: car care and usage; chores; transportation; general school and social activities; walls, their treatment and decoration; utilities and their usage; problems of the yard; clothes; and allowances.

Divide the problems, divide the responsibility. Find out which adult is most directly affected by the physical needs or results of the problem. Decide who is most qualified through expertise, interest, or personality to handle it.

It wasn't extraordinary for Clif to have known the mileage on the car that night he and Della tangled. He kept meticulous records of everything. He was orderly and precise, trained in facts, cost estimates, and actuality. Into his hands went those items that would benefit from his talents, natural personality, and training, as well as those problems which directly affected him.

On the other hand, after my years of full-time mothering, we decided I could best handle those problems residing in the gray areas, those requiring current knowledge of adolescent behavior, and those whose results directly affected me.

Don't try to assign everything. Even though some problems appear regularly, they may not fit a family rule, or happen the same way twice. For us, these included unexpected transportation requests, clutter in the house, extended bedtimes, sibling squabbles, and spur-of-the-moment permissions.

It helped us to assume, when both parents were present, that the adult most directly affected by the request or the behavior of the moment would handle it. If only one parent was present, that parent had the right to resolve the question to his/her satisfaction alone. If at times a youngster felt this was unfair, we reminded ourselves we were working on a process of growth, not a scientific formula for dispensing justice.

• Support Your Partner •

Just because you've divided problems and designated authority, it doesn't mean you'll always agree with your mate's handling of a situation. You didn't before, and your children knew it, and used it to their advantage. The above steps are just the beginning.

Consider the concerns of each parent. Clif and I each had legitimate concerns we were afraid would not be taken into consideration if we totally relinquished responsibility of certain situations to the other person.

Clif believed in instant consequences once a youngster had been given reasonable teaching and learning opportunities. I had trouble with this, and was overly generous with warnings and second chances. While we were both, in general, against physical discipline, at the time we decided to change our parenting process Clif still felt it had its place on occasion.

Be confident of the need for change. While preparing a talk for a group of parents, I found research supporting our own experiences. It is not good for children to be the divisive element that brings about open arguments between parents. Nor is it good for parents to react to each other or their children with emotional outbursts, such as face-slapping and hitting, or the uncontrolled yelling that creates intense anger and hostility.

Research also indicates that children thrive when the rights of both parents and children are honored: When parents set clear standards, make rules, and expect mature behavior from their children. This same approach encourages an open communication between the parent and child that permits verbal give-and-take and may result in changing rules and expectations. The most effective parents give love, show caring, value individuality and uniqueness, but do not rush to give a child adult privileges and freedom.

The research made sense to Clif and me. Assigning authority for certain problems seemed to give us room for holding the fort, while still giving our adolescents opportunities to initiate change. The new process definitely permitted the designated, most qualified person to focus his attention on situations he believed were important.

Continue communicating. Not in the old way of discussing every problem specifically, but now in a more general, all-encompassing manner: "What can you handle, what can't you handle?"

Clif and I talked about our size, strength, and the children's increasing ability to provoke us both to anger. I shared with him how even the possibility of physical contact between an angry adult and a rebellious adolescent kept me overly sensitive to family situations.

He, on the other hand, thought my hesitancy about letting our children experience the consequences of their behavior, or his displeasure, made me a buffer between him and them. At times, he felt I was undercutting the validity of his position.

With those thoughts in mind, we decided:

- Physical action, or even the threat of it, would no longer be an option for us.
- Clif would attempt to be more flexible, and I, less predictable.
- We'd be more tolerant of each other's efforts.
- We'd attempt to limit our use of threats, orders, and punishment, and strive instead for cooperation.
- If all else failed, we'd use the minimum, rather than the "deserved," consequence and make it as directly applicable to the offense as possible.

• Coping with Anger and Fear •

Our oldest son Mike was still in high school when Clif, en route home by car, passed him riding behind a friend on an oversized motorcycle. With reckless speed, they were weaving in and out of traffic and waving to friends on the sidewalk. Clif was furious.

Later he told me, "When I saw Mike, I couldn't believe it. After all our talks, and our rule about riding on motorcycles! I was out of the car and heading toward him by the time they turned the corner. I wanted to grab him, shake him, hit him, but on the way there I began pounding my fist into my hand and thinking about what we were trying. It helped. I didn't touch him. Instead, my anger all came out in words: How he could have been killed or paralyzed, or caused someone else to have a wreck." He shook his head, his pain and anger still showing. "I told him everything I felt like doing, including grounding him for the rest of the year, but all I did was ground him until I could think."

Clif had originally handled the motorcycle incident, so after further discussion with our son, he followed up with, "No riding the school bus for a week. You walk both ways and think about where you'd be if your legs were broken or paralyzed."

Tuesday night, Mike caught me in the kitchen and complained bitterly. "This doesn't make sense. I have tennis practice every day and a competition on Friday. I'm tired, loaded with books and homework, and I have to walk miles while the bus is half empty and my bike is sitting in the garage."

"It could be worse," I answered righteously.

His face hardened. "Well, I won't do it. I'll hitchhike or quit the team!"

"Oh, no, you won't! What you did was serious, terrible. You'll take your medicine or. . . . " Suddenly, I stopped. There I was involved, angry, ready with my threats and policing.

I put up my hand. "Wait, let me think." This was Clif's problem with his son. He didn't need me speaking for him. But hitchhiking was dangerous, and sports were this son's big thing. Still, he'd risked his life on the motorcycle and he could do it again and not be caught.

Did I want safety for this week, participation in sports for this year, or something more? I groaned inwardly and longed for a magic wand.

Then Mike's patience ran out. "Mom, say something, don't just look at me!"

Suddenly, my new awareness began to carry over from one situation to another. Mike was the one who would be directly affected by the threats he was presenting and he was the only one who could let the consequence result in his learning.

Slowly I began: "I need to take back what I just said. You can hitchhike, or even ride the bus, and we'd not know. We want your safety and obedience, but our wanting it isn't enough. You can also quit the team. We don't want that either. But the choices are yours to make. You are the one they will directly affect."

This wasn't the first time I had threatened a child through my fear, but it was the first time I acknowledged a child's greater power than mine over his actions.

Mike shrugged his shoulders and muttered as he turned, "Guess I'll talk to Dad after dinner. Maybe he'll let me walk a couple of the days next week instead."

Oh, joy! I didn't have to play God in this situation, protect our child at all costs, enforce Clif's discipline, or combat our son's threats. The matter was between the two of them, and our son's athletic life and safety were in his own hands.

• Two's a Team, Three's a Crowd •

That night, Clif and I realized, to our mutual delight, we'd each handled our part in the motorcycle situation better than usual. Assigning parent ownership and responsibility for problems was helping, but also, each of us had been alone with our son when we talked.

Would my behavior have gone so quickly from anger to reason if Clif had been present? What about Clif and our son's behavior that first day? What would have happened if Clif had grabbed Mike by the arm and, in all his anger, marched him into the house for a united parents' conference?

At any time it's easy for a third person to demonstrate with a word, or facial expression, his or her differing view. In the stress of family conflict, it's almost automatic for a parent to indicate his or her personal feelings with body posture, a raised eyebrow, or an innocent-sounding question.

Even if the youngster doesn't gain in that particular skirmish, the parent's area of sensitivity has been touched and his/her reaction noted. The specific point that has placed one parent's wisdom in question, and momentarily given the child the other person's support, is stored and available for use again.

One adult, one child, in a private place. The words ring with fairness. A loving parent, wanting to resolve a problem with a child, does not need the power brought by numbers.

During adolescence, the motivation to win is acutely high. Being found wrong means not only possible discipline, but loss of face and dignity. Before a discussion begins, it is easy to suggest moving to a private room or, if that's impossible at the moment, to delay the discussion until you can.

Refusal to discuss personal or controversial issues and conflicts in front of others (including grandparents, siblings, and friends) had a positive, instant effect on our household. Privacy seemed to encourage honesty and cooperation; small problems began to stay small and big ones to diminish in size.

In the rest of this book, you will see the experiences of this chapter become a cornerstone for our family's growing commitment to individual responsibility, dignity, power, and freedom of choice.

Divide and Communicate

• Steps to Change •

Identify adolescent situations that create problems between adults. Consider what you want your teen to learn through solving the problems. Divide those you agree can be handled by one adult.

Assign adult responsibility. Identify the adult who is most directly affected by an area of concern and best qualified to handle it. Openly acknowledge that adult's authority.

Be alert to audience influence. Have all discussions in a private place with one child and one adult present. A listening other person is always a potential ally or adversary to an adolescent. Privacy encourages honesty and cooperation.

Communicate adult to adult. Respect each other's emotional limits. Listen from the other person's position and feelings. Look for creative solutions.

Remember the research. No one benefits when children become divisive elements between parents. Children function best in homes where the rights of both parents and children are honored.

4

Natural Consequences

New Belief: *Our children want health, happiness, and success for themselves as much as we want these for them.*

• Higher Risk Consequences •

If you're experimenting in your home with the ideas I've presented thus far, you're now considering problems by asking yourself: "Who is directly affected by the results? Who should be thinking about how to solve the problem? Who has the power to make the solution work?" In other words, you've been identifying who owns the problem and then attempting to let the owner resolve it.

You have identified some minor problems, and have decided to let your child experience the consequences of his behavior in these areas, without your interference. However, being responsible is a complex skill learned as a result of making innumerable choices and living with the consequences. Our children will miss out on the very experience they must have to become responsible if we only allow them the learning on no-risk, low-cost opportunities.

First, we'll look at what our children have been gaining from our efforts to solve their problems. Then we'll consider what happens when parents step out of their problem-solving role and allow natural consequences to teach their children.

• Negative Words and Our Child's Self-Image •

Every time we respond to our children, they receive not only our attention for the concern of the moment, but spoken and unspoken messages about how we perceive them in general ways. These subtle messages are character forming.

Your daughter has not brought her gym clothes home to be washed for weeks. You insist she bring them Friday, or else. She doesn't, and the words pour out of your mouth: "I can't believe your carelessness, your lack of pride, your forgetfulness! Monday it was your math book, Wednesday the key to the house, and now you'll go another week to gym class smelling like a dirty clothes hamper!"

Does your criticism change her behavior? No. Saturday she leaves the stove burner on and no one notices for an hour. Now your comments reach farther: "Don't you care about safety, your family, our home? If you can't be responsible in such a simple matter as this, how can I trust you on the school camp-out?"

Have you ever felt you had a tape running in your head as you deal with a particular child? One that flips on with accusations and judgment despite your resolve to handle problems with such a child differently?

Children and parents who get into a judgmental position are usually in conflict in many areas. The child lies, confuses issues, and often seems to deliberately undermine the adult's efforts to improve or change the situation. Parents sometimes report: "We feel so helpless. We spend more time on this child than all our others, yet she's the least cooperative, responsible, or happy. Nothing we do seems to work!"

Most authorities acknowledge that for a child to grow emotionally, he or she needs: (1) A regular, caring involvement with at least one important adult. (2) Recognition of his unique value and worth to that adult. (3) A sense of having considerable choice and control over the circumstances that affect him.

Let's say a child brings home a warning notice and we respond angrily, "You're the only one in the family who doesn't keep up with his school responsibilities. Every quarter you get grounded for something! Get out your homework! We'll take one problem at a time, and maybe with me at your elbow every night, you won't goof off."

Our child's negative behavior triggers our involvement, we give a negative response and, to a high degree, the needs of both parent and child are met. We're paying attention, caring, and communicating. We've taken action and our tension and frustration subside for a few minutes. We're doing our best to make our child change, shape up, and succeed.

Yet, for our children negative attention is a waterwheel that raises all kinds of emotions that are not growth producing. The time, care, and attention they get from their poor behavior meet their needs, to some degree, for adult recognition and involvement. In choosing to misbehave, they experience a sense of control. Even if the results of their choices create problems, they have made choices and they defend them.

In the case of the gym clothes, the child knows she is guilty as charged, yet we hear: "I couldn't help it. The gym was locked." "It was raining." "The teacher let us out late and I'd have missed my bus." Excuses can be as varied and endless as the situation requires.

Still, these youngsters often believe they're doing their best. They listen to lectures, accept discipline, cry over our angry words and their inability to please. They tell us, and their friends, of their difficult life: How their work is never good enough, their teachers are the worst, and their stepparent hates them. Eventually the magnitude of their trials gives them status and identity within themselves and with their peers.

• The Fallacy of Parental Power •

Obviously, children do not get themselves into such a defensive position on purpose, nor do parents encourage it deliberately. Dealing with the problems of life in negative ways happens over time as parents assume they are responsible for solving their children's problems.

A child's first years in school often set the pattern for negative response. The first time we get a call from the elementary school teacher, we react. We lecture, schedule the child's study time, and make sure the work is completed satisfactorily. If this is an occasional situation, our child usually responds to the attention by getting back on track. If she continues to perform satisfactorily, we have no problem.

Unfortunately, some parents have a great deal of experience with teacher conferences, detention, and weekend assignment sheets. These parents have been supervising the school and home details of their children's academic careers for years with some success. Now, however, many find their efforts do not produce the results they once did when their children were in elementary school.

You might be a parent in such a situation. You know homework is important, and yet, despite all your efforts, your capable child still forgets to turn in the paper you helped her complete at midnight. Or, another child with a notice about failing math skips his tutoring appointment and is watching television when you get home.

The same kind of negative response exists in other areas of life. The umbrella you insisted your daughter carry is left with her lunch on the porch, and the care she promised to give her new pet is now *your* daily chore.

Our parental ability to control our children's behavior is only as effective as they are willing for it to be.

As noted before, almost any kind of parental discipline can change a child's behavior some of the time. However, our success is dramatically affected by: (1) The child's belief in her ability to accomplish what we wish. (2) The value the youngster places on what she has to gain, lose, or suffer in the process. (3) The intensity of an adolescent's desire for freedom from parental control at any given time.

Even with success, who gets the credit for accomplishment? The responsible parent or the child with his effort? Who *should* get the credit? We parents do not want to be like the seal trainer, who, with his presence and a fish, ensures the success of each performance. *Our aim is to make ourselves unnecessary to our child's success.*

Your child has heard you state repeatedly what you value and want for him. You have modeled the effort you'll put into reaching a goal and the emotional energy you'll apply to a problem's resolution. Isn't it time now for your child to consider what he values and desires—what he is willing to work to achieve?

You know this is true, but instantly, fear touches you. "Couldn't the results of wrong choices be too serious? What about their self-esteem, health, opportunities for sports, and college chances?"

Yes, but will risking the child's taking the natural consequences for his behavior be less threatening next year? Will you have more control and more influence over your child's behavior when she is in high school? Do you think your children will be listening more to adults when they're older? *Most probably, they will not.*

If fear is the problem, reassure yourself. You're not turning your youngster loose on life without adequate preparation. You've spoken, lectured, threatened, or disciplined your sons or daughters in regard to all the problems that you are now turning over to them. They can quote verbatim your deepest values and most heartfelt goals for them. They know your wisdom. Isn't it time to let natural consequences teach them?

• What Are Natural Consequences? •

I define a *natural consequence* as the outcome of a process whereby a youngster experiences the direct results of his behavior, impartially and naturally, through the normal flow of events. The consequence results from the child's behavior and the actions or reactions of adults other than his parents, his environment, and life situations.

Natural consequences are always effective because they are life-given, reality-based experiences. They cannot be set up by a parent. They can only happen through the natural process of circumstances and life.

As adults, we continue to learn daily through natural consequences. Yet, as good parents, we seem to feel we must not let our children experience the instructive results of their own behavior. We protect them. We keep their calendars current with test dates and activity times. We underline in red and post reminding notes on doors and mirrors. When our children still don't follow through, we step in, angry and powerful, and say, "You'll improve that grade or it won't be just an F on your report card! There'll be no ski trip!"

Natural consequences are most effective when there's no lecturing, advising, or threatening by parents and when the results are accepted without parental anger, punishment, or recriminations.

The adult's position is to be a listening, caring support to the youngster as he meets the life experience. Your child will be upset on occasion. With the absence of your blame or hindsight wisdom, you will have given your child space to share with you his disappointment in himself, what he may have learned, and perhaps how he will put the pieces together and use them as a stepping stone.

• How to Use Natural Consequences •

Plan ahead. Start with one or two situations you consider fitting and reasonable for your child's age and where the consequences aren't more than you can tolerate.

Behavior	Consequence
Doesn't do homework	Receives lower grade
Leaves clothes on floor	Clothes not clean when needed
Doesn't dress appropriately	Suffers illness or embarrassment
Forgets trip permission slip	Misses trip
Leaves bike out at night	Bike rusts or gets stolen
Fights in bus line	Walks or bikes to school
Drops a sport midseason	Coach and/or friends angry

Be prepared to suspend judgment and helpful suggestions. Watch yourself practice becoming the reasonable parent you've always wanted to be, not one controlled by your child's emotions or ego.

Bestow power. Children need it. They have it. Acknowledge it. Stop the battle and give generously. Think of your youngster as being genuinely concerned about his life and wanting to handle it. Plan to convey this message, as well as your altered view of your role in his problems.

For example, you might say: "I talk too much about your weight and you must hate it. I wouldn't want you or anyone else telling me when and what to eat. You're perfectly capable of making these decisions for yourself and I need to remember it. I won't be giving you smaller servings of dessert than the others, unless you specifically request it. It's your weight and your body, and you're capable of managing both."

Practice healthy neglect. Overlook the lunch left conspicuously on the bookcase and ignore the unwashed skirt you know she needs to wear tomorrow. As she talks with friends of new plans, resist reminding her about the appointment for her haircut. Avoid asking how he's managed without his school books or gym clothes.

If in the past you've met your youngster at the door with heartfelt interest and concern shining across your face—change your behavior. Allow your child to seek you in her time. Let him choose his place for telling, then listen more, talk less, and keep your responses low-key. When your overweight child steps on the scales, move away and get intensely involved in something else. Do not ask what the scales said. Avoid information-seeking questions and those that can be answered with only a yes or no.

Questions often convey judgment and the idea that if parents know the facts, they can improve the situation. This creates a false ownership of the problem.

Some children will find being newly responsible intoxicating and addictive. Others will be worried and afraid, doubting their ability to handle all the power, or your ability to relinquish it.

Stand in their shoes. Some of our youngsters try to get us back into our old position of responsibility by exaggerating the problem and predicting their own downfall. Maybe you've just come in from work and you hear of your child's terrible conference with his seventh-grade teacher. He says, "I hate school. I'm six papers behind in social studies and there's no way I can do them by Friday!"

You want him to learn something, so you respond to feelings, accept his threats, and view the problem from his position. You don't lecture. You don't talk about how he could have prevented this from happening. Picture yourself as a friend, standing beside your child, hearing the difficulties, but with no need to act or change anything.

Acknowledge the problem as real. "You've always been able to make up what you were missing, but now six papers! That's rough."

"She should have told me sooner," he moans. "There's no way I can finish my report and do those, too! So I get an F, so that's it for sports! I don't care, school stinks. It doesn't matter if I flunk!"

Good! Now he's feeling natural, God-given anxiety about a situation that affects his life. Don't weaken the impact. Self-placed anxiety from a natural consequence is tremendously motivational.

In the past when he's felt anxiety, he's shared it, and then you felt anxious too. You probably began to generate solutions, offer help, deliver discipline, or promise rewards. Not now. Continue rephrasing his words, picking up his main points, and recognizing his resentment and frustration.

Remember, the acknowledgment of feelings can be expressed often with just your touch, a nod, a caring murmur, and the love on your face.

Recognize choices. In the middle of all this turmoil, your youngster may come up with a totally new problem. In such a situation Matt, then a sixth grader, suddenly suggested his transferring for the second semester to the middle school where I worked. He'd been thinking about this for weeks, for reasons other than his grades. I hadn't suspected. We need to respect our youngster's thinking on any solution and explore with him or her its possibilities and problems.

Avoiding taking the responsibility for resolving the problem doesn't mean avoiding a discussion about it.

Use new communication. Avoid judgmental statements, anxiety, and commonsense suggestions. You want your youngster to do most of the thinking and talking. When he asks, "Why do I have to study that?" Answer the question with a question, "Hmmm, why should you?"

Consider seriously any response. If he asks, "Do I have to?" you answer, "I don't know. What do you think will happen if you don't?" Or, "How important is it to you to take a stand on this?" "What are the advantages and the disadvantages each way?"

He threatens. You answer by summarizing what he's given as an option and acknowledge it is a choice he can make. You might talk about the worst that can happen, his power to let it happen or not, and his and your ability to handle the possible outcomes.

She's belligerent and uncooperative. Try reading her body language. "You're so angry you want to scream, not talk." Stay with your child's position, don't rush the talk and problem solving. Later paraphrase, summarize, and explore options.

Honor the dilemma. Recognize the difficulty of deciding and be willing to live without the resolution of the problem. Allow your child time to experience his control of the situation and think about the possible consequences. The child who wanted to move to my school talked of it off and on all evening. At bedtime he asked me to wake him when I awoke at 5:30 A.M. "In three mornings I can catch up. I don't want to take an F to your school."

Respect their decisions. A week later, with all his late work in, and permission granted from my school district for the transfer, he said, "I don't think I'll change schools. Having to travel on your schedule would be worse than letting a couple of little kids get away with their name calling and teasing. I'm so tall they call me a bully if I chase them, and a chicken if I don't, but I'll figure out something."

• Natural Consequences Are Food for Growth •

A genuine belief in the value of natural consequences and a caring, accepting participation in allowing them to occur quickly brings returns. You'll notice your child thinking about her life, giving attention to its details, and creatively taking responsibility for making it run well.

Often you'll smile inside as you see your child doing what needs to be done for his own comfort and happiness and you'll begin to marvel at his ingenuity and management skills.

You'll notice an unexpected relaxation in yourself and an immunity to unproductive game playing. You'll see old set-in-concrete response patterns disappearing. You'll worry less and trust more. You'll know again real, on-the-job parent satisfaction!

Matt was in the eighth grade when I first enjoyed those wonderful feelings of completely trusting the process.

He came in from school, his face furious as he slammed his books onto the table. "I've just lost my A in Spanish! In one minute from an A to a C!"

Obviously there was more to the story than one sentence conveyed, but I had to remember, grades belong to him. *Respond to the information given and feelings shown.* "How awful! From an A to a C in Spanish, your best class!"

"Not any more! I didn't go to Spanish Friday because of a student council meeting, so I didn't get reminded about the two pages of memorized dialogue we do every grading period. I was the first one he called on this morning!"

He turned suddenly and pounded the wall with his fist. "He called on me on purpose. It could have been tomorrow. I'm the only student representative in his class. I can't believe it! A zero, one third of my report card grade and he doesn't even care!"

Distance yourself. For an instant, words of recrimination and advice played through my mind, then like a wave of nausea they were gone. This was his world and I didn't have the knowledge to enter it.

It was a brand new feeling for me—one that distanced me from him, putting space between us physically and emotionally. My love and concern were still there, but any personal involvement or need to act or speak to the situation was missing.

I shook my head, "You must feel just sick about it."

"Yeah, and what good does it do? He just told me to tell the class the rule." His shoulders dropped. "Of course, I knew about checking with him or a friend on what happens during a class. I just forgot.

"Mom, I went in after school, and he still wouldn't talk about it! Just shook his head and told me I should have remembered the rule!"

With that, our son belligerently shoved his books to the floor, swore, and headed to his room, slamming doors on the way.

Resist fall-out! If Matt had been our first youngster, I'm sure I would have jumped up instantly, full of parental indignation and input, and shouted, "You don't have to yell and swear! It was your own fault! Come back and pick up these books . . . and don't slam doors!"

He kicked his trash can, pounded the wall, and swore some more. I'd never seen Matt so upset over anything! Yet I wasn't upset. I could hardly believe it.

In a few minutes, I heard him throwing the basketball against the garage doors. Wham, wham, wham; then, bounce, bounce, into the hoop; wham, wham, doors; bounce, bounce, hoop. For ten minutes it went on, then total quiet.

Suddenly, he was back. "Mom, I know what I'm going to do." His eyes were shining and his face alive and eager. "I'll memorize the dialogue tonight, go in before school tomorrow and tell Mr. M. what I've done, and ask him if he'll give me half credit if I say it perfectly!"

I was stunned. The words just popped out, "What if he doesn't? It's so much to learn!"

"I thought about that, but it's my only chance."

The next morning the teacher listened to his recitation, and said, "Not half credit, 80 percent. Effort beyond the call of duty deserves consideration of the same kind!"

Oh, what this man-child learned about himself that day. Yet if I, by some miracle, had thought of that idea and dared to suggest it, how do you think he would have responded?

Someday, after watching yourself keep out of a situation that would have previously entangled you up to your neck, and then seeing your child do more to solve his problem than you'd ever have thought or dared to ask of him, you'll know that self-discipline thrives in an atmosphere free from judgment and blame.

In the next chapter, we'll be working with *logical* consequences and how they help us parents take care of the problems we do own.

Natural Consequences

• Steps to Change •

Trust the growth process. Recognize your teenager's strong internal drive towards positive and independent functioning. Realize that your ability to determine your teen's behavior is only as effective as she is willing for it to be.

Appreciate natural consequences. They are your child's best teachers. You do not cause them and you can't arrange them, but your behavior can influence their effectiveness. Work on that.

Announce your position. Choose a problem that carries some risk. Acknowledge in a friendly manner your child's ownership and your changed view of your position.

Move into neutral. Step back emotionally from your child and the problem. Be interested and understanding, but not anxious. Don't try to lessen the results natural consequences bring.

Become a responsive listener. Acknowledge the problem. Give attention to facts, feelings, and choices. Respect the difficulty of decision making. Do not push for solutions, action, and commitment.

5

Parent-Owned Problems

New Belief: *There are lessons of living that children must learn if they are to function successfully within their family and community. Effective parents teach those lessons in a relationship-building, growth-producing manner.*

• Identifying Parent-Owned Problems •

You have already made a list of the things your child does that cause you concern and end with you judging her behavior and trying to get the problem resolved. You then established ownership of the various problems by looking at your child's behavior in light of three questions:

- Who do the results of the situation directly affect in the long run?
- Who should be thinking about how to solve the problem?
- Who has the power to make the solution succeed?

A few of the problems may have ended with your name answering each question. If so, these are clearly parent-owned problems. With other concerns, some of the questions were undoubtedly answered with your child's name and yours.

In a situation where ownership is shared, it is important to identify the part or parts that do directly affect you, and consider specifically those parts you can resolve. We'll be talking about parts of problems later in this chapter as we consider some of the more difficult situations parents face in rearing adolescents.

Now take your list of problems and look at those you have

marked with your name. They may include some of the following: doesn't do chores; is defiant and disrespectful at home or in public; disobeys rules of curfew and activities; abuses furniture, telephone rights, television and food privileges; uses other people's clothes and jewelry without permission; and has friends over when parents aren't home.

You can see that each of these concerns directly affects a parent and therefore the parent has the responsibility for working toward a satisfactory resolution of the problem, or else changing her attitude toward it.

By now, most of us recognize the limitations and ineffectiveness of solutions gained through parental power and control. Later on we'll talk about insights and attitude changes. For now, we'll be considering the use of new communication skills and logical consequences for gaining our children's cooperation.

• Shifting Your Position •

During our children's early years we automatically put them first, focusing on their needs and desires, and operating on their time schedule. Our love relieved their hurts and our wisdom resolved their problems. They appreciated our care, returned our affection, and tried to please us. No wonder we developed the idea that this was the way it was supposed to be forever.

However, as adolescence approaches, things change. Their requests become demands and our efforts go unappreciated. As their independence increases, ours seems to decrease.

We want their cooperation, but we get their resistance. It seems every situation begins with an argument and ends with anger and threats. Such situations repeated routinely in a family discourage parents and build poor behavior patterns in children. Fortunately, we can improve behavior and end discouragement by changing the way we handle those problems that belong to us.

Begin by putting some distance between you and your child. Start with situations that directly affect you, but do not need the young person's cooperation for their success. You need this practice if you are to be able to communicate your needs and desires to your children in a clear and friendly manner on situations that do require their cooperation.

Use "I" statements relating to your own life when you talk to your youngsters. "I" statements reflect and indicate self-responsibility. "You" statements judge and carry blame. What you'll be doing now is practicing out loud your right to be you: To feel as you feel, think your thoughts, plan your time, and fulfill your desires.

Serve an outlandish flavor of ice cream or an unusual kind of lunch meat. When someone complains, smile, and in a friendly tone say, "Yes, and I love it. I'm spoiling me today." When you're accused of favoring one sibling over another, accept the complaint lightly and acknowledge your ability to be influenced by a good deed. "Hmm, maybe your brother *is* my favorite today. I'll love driving the car he just washed."

Practice unpredictability. Rearrange furniture, be silly if you've been serious, schedule a play instead of a movie, or plan an out-of-the-ordinary Saturday. Get a new hair style and don't ask for anyone's opinion. If they give it, accept it casually. You are pleasing you. If you're in the habit of checking with your children about their unscheduled plans before making some of your own—don't. Start a new hobby. Change routines.

Accept their negative responses. If you give a child a chance to participate in an activity and he groans, accept it immediately as his wish not to participate. **Never try to talk an adolescent into accepting your ideas and plans for fun.** Once you do, you've entered a parent prison, one that holds you responsible for your child's happiness and the success of the activity.

Develop a new vocabulary. Begin to use words that reflect your rights and the responsibility you're now considering for your well-being. "I feel, I will, I want, I think, I like . . ." "I like red; I'll take five red balloons." "I want the den tonight between eight and ten. I feel happy and I've rented a happy video." After she says your choice of a movie stinks, hear yourself saying, "Maybe so, but I think I'll like it." Then watch it and enjoy it.

Our children do not usurp our time, energy, and rights: We give these to our children. So we also have the ability to take them back.

Check your position and attitude. Remember, you do have the right to have your belongings respected, the house settled at a given time, and your home not used by others without your permission. You have a right to be treated with courtesy and have your time, plans, and concerns considered. You do your child no favor if he or she is not certain of your commitment to taking care of yourself.

Decide what is bothering you most. Is it someone tying up the telephone for hours, leaving the tub dirty after every bath, or bringing home undesirable friends when you're not there?

Whatever the issue, you will be using the following problem-solving setting and three-part statement as your basic tools.

• Communicate Your Position •

Choose a setting with one parent, one child, in a private place. Be prepared to communicate openly, courteously, and calmly with your youngster about your wants and needs.

Plan to use a three-part sentence stating what has happened, how you feel about it, and why you feel this way. Your focus will be on "I" messages.

1. Describe exactly what you see or what has happened in factual or behavioral terms, "When I come home and find wet towels on the bed . . ."
2. A statement of how you feel about this, "I am concerned (upset, worried) . . ."
3. Tell why you feel this way, "because I know it's bad for the electric blanket and the mattress."

———

Note how concisely this simple, reasonable statement brings a problem into focus without placing blame or guilt. Of course, on the first try you'll get instant reassurance. "No problem. I'll be careful."

Then a few days later you're faced with the same situation, as I was with my daughter Barbara.

• Work for Resolution •

Next time, same setting and plan, but use a stronger message. "When, despite your good intentions, wet towels continue to end up on bedroom furniture, I get upset. I know it's bad for the bed and it seems unfair that my needs aren't being given the attention they deserve. I want your help."

Depending upon your child's response and how you've dealt with this before, you may want to ask, "Is there a bigger problem here than just wet towels—something I don't know about?"

Be prepared to listen to your youngster's words of defense and respond to the facts and feelings as stated. Our daughter, Barbara, looked surprised. "No, I just forget because someone's always in the bathroom by the time I finish with my hair. I *do* dry my hair in the bedroom."

"You're right," I answered, really understanding her position. "Drying your hair in your bedroom is a big thing. I'd really not understood you were doing that regularly. I know it makes a difference in good use of bathroom time."

However, because it's a parental problem, we see it to resolution. "Still I guess I'd like to have everything: Your effort beyond the call of duty, and the wet towel problem handled in a better (fairer, more satisfactory or manageable) way."

Often with this kind of communication going on, many of her personal needs may have been met through your listening and the way you've approached the situation. If so, there's a good chance she will come up with a suggestion that will resolve the problem.

She does, it works for a week, then you find wet towels on the dresser. What now? One option is to continue the problem solving. Another is the use of logical consequences which we will cover in a moment.

• The Democratic (Shared Responsibility) Way •

Remember your commitment. Using the same problem-solving setting as before, you now state with another firm, calm "I" message your claim to your own needs, and your belief that basic fairness will bring about a change in your child's behavior.

My son and I disagreed about his friends' visiting in our home: "When I continue to see signs you've been having friends in the house when I'm away, I'm concerned. I know you can't control their behavior and I worry about someone getting hurt or our belongings damaged. I don't think it's fair for me to go to work feeling insecure about what's happening here. For my peace of mind, I want us to resolve this."

Angrily, he answered, "You just don't like my friends, Mom, face it!"

React with sincerity and honesty. "Yes, I guess it could seem I'm trying to keep you from being with your friends. I admit seeing them smoking pot in the park has added to my concern. Still, it's always been a rule: No one but family in the house until I'm home. I want your help in resolving this."

Continue to listen, clarify, and summarize. Paraphrase his words, excuses, and complaints. If they're complicated or he brings up new concerns, ask him to stop for a moment so you can tell him in your own words what he's just said about the situation and his feelings. If it is you doing the talking, ask, "Will you tell me in your words how I feel about this situation?"

Seek solutions with his cooperation. "Still, I want a better way of handling this, and I want us to think of something that will work." Explain that there will be no evaluation of solutions at this stage, just brainstorming ideas. Give him time to contribute his ideas before offering yours. If none are forthcoming, suggest you both think and meet again at a specified time. Do not let this stage be taken lightly. You must be serious about problem resolution and your youngster must see it in your behavior.

Write down suggestions. You and your youngster eliminate the ones that obviously won't work and discuss the others. Settle on the solution you both think has the greatest possibility for working. Sometimes two poor ideas combined can resolve everything.

Plan a follow-up talk. Choose a definite time and date for talking about how the solution is working. Mark it on your calendar. You do not want good intentions to be lost in the confusion of a holiday season or visit from friends. Neither do you want to forget to notice and appreciate changed behavior.

Still, the best plan may not work. You may come home early and find your son and his friends in the living room watching TV, throwing a basketball back and forth, and eating. The use of a logical consequence is an option you have.

• Logical Consequences •

Logical consequences are different from natural ones. They involve the parent either setting up a situation that pertains to, and follows, a child's particular behavior or else involves the parent withdrawing his or her participation from a situation so other natural consequences may occur.

• Logical consequences are not punishments. They indicate that a child has a choice. He may continue the behavior and continue to take the consequence, or change his behavior and not have a consequence.

• Logical consequences do not have to equal in severity the ongoing behavior. You are simply giving your youngster a message that says for fairness, order, or your well-being, you cannot let the behavior continue unnoted and without consequences.

• Logical consequences should not carry messages of anger and blame. In fact, they must be used in a calm, nonpunitive, uncontrolling manner to be effective.

• Logical consequences are not effective in every situation. You are problem solving and this requires the parent's position and feelings to be openly acknowledged and discussed.

• Logical consequences are not written in stone. They are tailored to handle individual parent, child, family, and community needs with all kinds of room for change and adjustment.

————

For the wet towel situation, you might move a drying rack into the child's room and place it on a piece of scrap linoleum, or install rods on bedroom doors, or place a plastic container for damp items in an acceptable spot. Explain that you understand about the bathroom situation, but since the furniture is suffering, this will relieve your concern for the moment.

If a son or daughter is having friends in your home without your permission, you have effective *logical consequences* available. You can hire a house sitter or pay a neighbor who is home to keep an eye on your youngster at their home during after-school hours. Obviously, this would limit the money you'd have left to spend on your child's recreation and extras.

A single parent decided her peace of mind at work demanded a strong show of her commitment to the proper use of her home. She shortened her working day by taking from her vacation time and arriving home early.

"I'll return to full-time work and accumulating vacation time for *our* summer trip when you feel you have the house and friend situation under control," she explained to her child. During the next two weeks, she and her son cleaned the garage, painted his

room, and made a garden. When they felt the problem was resolved, she returned to working a full day.

• Parental Withdrawal from a Situation •

The removal of a parent's participation in a situation allows
other *natural* consequences to take effect, also. A trip to the fabric store had been scheduled for immediately after my arrival home
one day. In the car, the casual, cotton dress material I understood
Ginny needed for her sewing class became a jersey-knit dress fabric for the eighth-grade graduation dance. Her first formal!

In one sentence, the simple shopping trip I'd envisioned had
turned into a monumental ordeal involving more money, options,
and decisions than I could handle. Using "I" messages as best I
could, I explained my inability to deal with this change on such
short notice, and my need to stay with our original plan.

Instantly, she was furious. "It's my class, my dress, and I'll be
doing the work. You just don't want to spend the money!" Her
voice rose as she began to review my weaknesses and failings as
a parent, my unfairness, and all the difficulties of her life as
an overworked and under-rewarded daughter with an uptight
counselor mother!

*Logical consequences must be related in a commonsense way
to the behavior.*

Suddenly, that great calmness I'd felt with our son and his
schoolwork came over me in this situation. I couldn't stop my
daughter's anger and her accusations, but I didn't have to be responsible for them. The class was hers. *I* didn't need the material
today.

At the next intersection, I made a U-turn and headed home.

"What's the matter? Where are we going?" she screamed.

"Home," I answered softly. "I'm sorry, but I don't think I'm
in any condition to continue with this trip today."

"But you promised! We had it on the calendar!"

"I know, but I can't do it. If I went now I'd be angry and
resentful and there's no way you'd want a mother like that on a
shopping trip."

Ginny leaned back in her seat, stunned. "I can't believe you're
doing this. I have to have my material tomorrow. What am I
going to tell my teacher?"

"I don't know. That's up to you."

We turned into our driveway and she exploded, "This is dumb, dumb, dumb! You're just punishing yourself. You'll have to take me eventually."

It didn't feel like punishment to me. It felt great! I wasn't angry, resentful, or even upset. *I was taking care of what I should be managing—my own feelings.* The rest was up to her.

I stopped the car and faced our daughter, "You're right, we will go out again. By then we'll have talked about everything and come to an agreement on what is to be bought."

• More Difficult Problems •

That's all very well for wet towels and shopping trips, but what do we do when a child regularly lies, cuts classes, and we're overwhelmed with calls and conferences? Or smokes cigarettes, uses drugs, circumvents discipline, and throws tantrums?

While all the problems above might seem to directly affect a parent, we actually have no power to stop a youngster from lying, having tantrums, using illegal substances when out of the house, or refusing to go to school. We've already tried making rules and enforcing discipline. Our child knows our concerns.

These and many other problems that indirectly affect us must be designated as belonging to our adolescent. So what do we do?

We recognize our limitations. Adolescent power is enormous. Many of our struggles with our teenagers are really our attempts to keep them safe, healthy, and out of legal trouble, in spite of themselves.

Unfortunately, no one likes being told what to do for their own good. Teenagers are no exception. In fact, we weaken our position with our children when we give them orders we can't enforce and they won't obey.

We look at our own behavior. Are there things we are doing that may be detrimental to our well-being or contrary to the values we're attempting to teach our children?

Our younger two were in early adolescence when I was asked to give a talk about the use of alcohol by middle-school age children. As I researched the subject, I realized we were giving our own children double messages about our values.

The alcohol that we said was only a beverage for celebrating special occasions, had, over the years, gradually become something else. It was the drink of relaxation, the wine that improved our home dinners and social events. For our returning adult children, as routinely as I bought them their favorite foods, I had the beer of their choice in the refrigerator.

The old adage, "Do as I say, not as I do," probably never did work. We need to change our behavior or our values when a conflict between the two is evident.

We get smart. We educate ourselves and our children. Our early adolescent is using pot, not daily, but certainly too often to consider it just experimenting. She denies it's harmful, rejects our advice and concern as old-fashioned, and makes promises she doesn't keep.

We visit our local school counselor and ask for the names of organizations, physicians, and counselors known to be working with parents and adolescents on controlling substance abuse.

We contact these resources and get their advice. We obtain the latest information available on the immediate and long-term effects of various drugs.

We use good skills and accurate information. We meet privately with our adolescent, describe the situation, and address our ongoing concerns. We acknowledge our lack of power in the situation, but indicate our desire to have her be well informed about the possible consequences of her decisions.

Depending upon our relationship with our adolescent, we may share credible information and literature on the subject with her. Or ask that she meet with a knowledgeable physician or counselor for further information on how the substance affects an adolescent physically, mentally, and legally.

We handle the parts that belong to us. The situation continues. We never ignore it. We meet again and again with our child and each time, *using the three-part sentence*, describe the problem in its latest form and the child's behavior. We may notice the red eyes, the hurried visits to the bathroom as soon as she comes home, the neglect of school and home duties, or the "It's no big deal" attitude we receive each time we talk about it to her.

We state our feelings and concerns calmly, but with words appropriate to our feelings and the seriousness of the behavior: "I hate your using a drug that affects your behavior now, and I worry about the physical and mental damage that doesn't show but may still be happening. I think about this a lot, but I know the decision is yours, not mine."

Then we take a deep breath, recognize she's made good decisions in the past and state our belief that, in the long run, she will choose what is best for her welfare on this. We say, however, "In the meantime, I want us to talk about the part (or parts) of the problem that are directly affecting your father and me, and require our decisions."

• Taking Care of Us •

We make rules for our well-being, not theirs. We cannot keep adolescents from smoking cigarettes, but we can choose not to have smoking in our home. When we know an older adolescent is smoking pot or using alcohol, a rule for our benefit would be no use of illegal substances. If he breaks the rule, a logical consequence would be to deny him the use of our car for social purposes.

Enforcing such a rule would give a strong statement to our child and his peers about our position against the use of drugs of any kind for our youngster. It would also protect us legally and financially from the consequences of their driving while under the influence of a drug.

We handle circumstances so that the consequences of our children's problem behavior fall as directly as possible on them and as indirectly as possible on us. Despite laws that mandate compulsory education, cutting school is almost an adolescent disease. With Mike, our first, we responded to notices of unexcused absences with angry, threatening words, grounding, and the withholding of privileges.

While his attendance improved temporarily, his adolescent drive towards excitement and independence did not lessen. At a later date, he and some friends cut school and on the spur of the moment became involved in activity that brought more serious consequences to all three.

We cannot force our adolescent children to obey the rules and laws set up for their protection and benefit. However, we can help them understand the realities of life and the importance of their choices when we:

- Engage our adolescent regularly in decision-making, problem-solving sessions that consider present, and possible future, effects of their behavior on us and them.
- Continue to search for solutions to ongoing problems, utilize logical consequences effectively, and seek expert advice.
- Support the natural consequences that come from the police, school, and other adult authorities.

With experience, Clif and I gradually developed confidence in openly recognizing with a youngster our inability to get his/her compliance on certain matters, but also expressing our need to react to the problem the behavior was creating for us and others.

With the next school-cutting incident, we decided any adolescent cutting school would spend an equal number of weekend hours cleaning, sanding, and painting house eaves, gutters, and the backyard fence. This is work that regularly needs doing and both sexes can do it well.

While we respect our children's needs and differences through cooperative problem solving, we also continue to identify the parental rights we want and commit ourselves to getting them. Most situations difficult to resolve involve parental rights that our child, his friends, other parents, the law, and experts recognize as valid.

You do have the right to have everyone share in home responsibilities; to live in security, order, and reasonable peace; to make plans and fulfill outside duties. Claiming these rights for yourself involves your open communication and commitment. Don't give up!

Your adolescent regularly forgets to turn off the light in his room. Make it a game. Explain that when the light is left on, you will unscrew the light bulb from the lamp and each time place it in a different bedroom drawer.

Neglected or forgotten household chores are a regularly irritating problem. Let all your children know the problems they create for you and that henceforth you will be reacting each time you have to remind someone of a task.

Then, in a private place, ask the next "delinquent" youngster to do the forgotten chore now and come back to you immediately. When she returns, have in mind a quick job you usually do yourself or one not assigned that day to anyone. She can clean the bathroom mirrors or the window over the kitchen sink. He might use the vacuum cleaner to dust the bookcase shelves and books or a dusty closet floor.

Remember, you are not punishing your youngster for forgetting, you are acknowledging your feelings and giving your child a definite message about a problem that continues to take your time unfairly.

• Give-and-Take in Life •

By recognizing your need for your child's cooperation in solving problems that affect you, and communicating with him accordingly, you take an important step in changing his behavior toward you. You can expect, and request, from your children a similar communication style when they want your cooperation in solving their problems.

The use of the processes we've covered in this chapter quickly improves relationships in a family. When you start taking care of yourself in a friendly, calm, and responsible manner, the value of give-and-take becomes apparent to an adolescent. Many of the things your young person has assumed are his rights are really privileges and he may need your help in recognizing which is which.

––––––

Later with Ginny, it was easy to suggest we discuss the sewing situation. We had time and we both knew I was not going to be forced into a decision I didn't want to make. I was open to her suggestions. She had seen me take care of myself without resorting to angry or derogatory comments, so she was able to hear my concerns. A give-and-take atmosphere had been established.

In the end, Ginny agreed to talk with her teacher about suitable materials and patterns for a beginning seamstress to turn into a formal, as well as the after-school help she might need to accomplish this.

We talked about the amount of money she would save by making her own dress and the hours of searching time I'd not have to give to shopping for a formal dress. We negotiated spending the saved dollars and both came away feeling pleased with ourselves.

The result of give-and-take is mutual satisfaction.

Parent-Owned Problems

• Steps to Change •

Check the give-and-take balance at your house. Do you feel your child frequently takes advantage of you and your goodwill? If so, change how you're handling problems that directly affect you.

Take responsibility for yourself. Become proficient in the use of "I" messages. Reclaim your independence, rights, and freedoms on situations that do not require your child's cooperation.

Seek your child's cooperation on situations that require it. With one adult and one child in a private place describe the situation, state how you feel, and why. Use the democratic problem-solving approach. Seek creative solutions.

Use logical consequences effectively to get your needs met. Do not allow a teenager to ignore the direct impact his behavior has on his parents' rights and freedoms.

Recognize your limitations in the face of difficult teen problems. Continue to communicate with your teen, identify your rights, and take care of them. Seek assistance from knowledgeable people. Respect your teenager's power and desire for self-responsibility.

6

Changing Our Attitudes

New Belief: *High expectations, when followed by criticism or angry words, give children overdoses of blame and guilt and leave them prisoners to their own inadequacies.*

• Can't You Do Anything Right? •

"You said you finished weeding. What do you call these?" "Look at this kitchen. You didn't wipe the counters and the sink needs scrubbing!" "Feel this floor. Do you call it clean?"

It seemed such words were our follow-up to almost every task. Chores were "forgotten," partially completed, or unacceptably done. Worst of all, some results were still unsatisfactory even after a callback and re-do.

Depending upon moods, tasks, and the parent-child relationship at the moment, kids respond to chores with excuses, dragging of feet, half-hearted repair jobs, and complaints. They tell us, "There's no pleasing you. You never see what's done, only what isn't." Then one day one of our teens added, "Mom, don't you get tired of putting so much time into our chores? You assign, we do. You check and scold, we argue. You lecture, we moan. Eventually we get the work done, only tomorrow you have to argue again with someone else!"

Chores are a major concern for most parents. Chores take on different shapes and sizes with each stage of development and require modifications and new solutions at every turn. In most homes, children's work is not an option, it's a given. Their work affects us directly, now and as long as they share our homes.

Seeing that the work is done is our responsibility and we even have the power to make our solutions work . . . well, some of the time with some of the youngsters they work.

Were my instant opinions and judgments a part of the work problem around our house? While Clif and I were becoming pretty sure that judgmental statements did not win cooperation, how could we take care of our massive household cleaning needs without criticism and correction? How would our children learn if we didn't hold them to our standards?

Most parents do not begin teaching children to do chores with criticism and correction. Initially we use reasonable expectations, helpful instruction, and parental praise and appreciation. We also think we will be as successful as we were when we taught our child to walk, talk, use silverware, throw a ball, and ride a tricycle. I recall reacting to a seven-year-old's "clean" kitchen with enthusiasm and accepting others' barely completed chores as well done. I felt fine about their performance; they were trying so hard.

Yet what are we to do a few years later when the children's efforts are conspicuously absent—when we can't miss the trash swept into the corner, the yard still marred by paths of high grass, the car washing that doesn't include the windows? What do we do when the words of praise feel so false we can't draw them from our throats?

• Developing the Spirit of Appreciation •

Clif and I talked of our concerns, but struggled on with the same basic approach until an exchange of comments with our daughter Teresa triggered new insights.

In all her adolescent self-righteousness, she declared, "I've just spent two hours making cookies for Matt's party! You walk in, Mom, glance around, thank me for making them, and in the next sentence ask me why I didn't include the top of the bookcase when I straightened the living room!"

She was right. Routinely, I acknowledged her best efforts with just a "thank you." I also said the same to the waiter, the mail carrier, and the telephone operator. I said "thanks" when the checker at the store gave me my change or someone blessed my sneeze.

Now, I expected those same overused words to express my

appreciation for her hours of intense personal effort. I further decreased their value by following them with the discouraging phrase, "But why didn't you . . . ?"

Nodding my head hard, I said, "Give me another chance. I'll go out and come in again." I had to grin at the funny look on her face. "It's okay, your dad and I are trying to learn a better way of communicating with you kids."

Outside I thought for a moment of the three-part sentence I'd been using when trying to change our children's problem behavior. Could it work with expressing appreciation? *Describe the situation, state feelings, tell why.*

I returned slowly and began, "When I see these chocolate-chip cookies, I don't see just cookies. I see you here, alone, mixing batter, filling cookie sheets, then watching batch after batch bake without burning." Now the words were there: "And I feel absolutely ecstatic and greatly loved because your brother's going to get homemade cookies for his school party, and I didn't have to make them!"

"That's good," she said, her face glowing after we'd hugged. "It almost makes me wish I'd cleaned the bookcase." Then she added contentedly, "You really do understand, don't you? All the time I was working I kept thinking how much this was going to mean to you. I know you feel sad when you can't do for the younger kids the things you used to do for the rest of us."

My heart soared! And to think, I almost missed this feeling because of a shoulder-high, room-divider bookcase that has a clean-life expectancy of about 15 minutes. How many other such opportunities were Clif and I missing?

Did we have tunnel vision when it came to chores and our children? Did we too often follow acknowledgment of what they had done immediately with what they had not?

I focused on chores. Is it really true that any job worth doing is worth doing well? Do I live by that rule in my work? Does anyone? Of course not—some tasks deserve no more than the old "lick and a promise" approach. Others, after forcing ourselves to do them for years, we find aren't worth doing at all. Remember ironing sheets and undershorts?

We also knew we couldn't justify our standards with the idea that we were forming in our children the housecleaning habits they'd use as adults. Della and her housemates, now away at college, were into pets, natural things, and health. They lived hap-pily in communal disarray.

Mike's older college group was worse. He and his friends bragged about their ground cover of weeds and their instant dish-*rinsing* which had replaced any need for dish-*washing!*

If such casual housekeeping could happen with two kids taught from an early age until the day they left home that "by one's work is the worker known," then possibly we had our priorities confused.

What happens as day after day we verbalize dissatisfaction or disapproval of our children's behavior? *Do our high expectations automatically create daily disappointment for everyone?* Is there a better way?

• The Elements of Change •

Attitude. Could I break my habit of fault-finding by not even expecting success on my first viewing of a child's work? If so, I could let my body and facial expressions indicate immediately my recognition of any small, positive improvement.

Words. Then, using the three-part sentence, I could describe what I saw and liked, express my pleasurable feelings and then stop, leave, or talk of something else. Later I could come back to anything that simply had to be addressed. This way I would be giving an honest, positive, first reaction and the youngster would have a chance of feeling it.

Practice. "Hey, no dishes on the kitchen table. I like coming home to that." "A driveway free of toys! I feel taken care of." "The roses are trimmed! I love seeing the wilted ones gone."

There was a new tone in my voice and I liked it. I began to notice all kinds of things: "How helpful to find the dryer empty, the milk I left out back in the fridge, the snack dishes in the dish-washer." A touch on an arm, a smile, and a nod of recognition for picking up spilled food immediately became a new part of my communication. I could feel my attention focusing on the positive rather than the negative and love flowing! Learning to express appreciation of many small things made my efforts easier than if I had tried to focus on the children's less numerous major accom-plishments.

Follow-up behavior. If on follow-up a chore still needed attention, I could use the same first two steps and add my position. "When I find the counter still cluttered and dirty with breakfast dishes, I feel frustrated because I can't begin dinner. I'll be upstairs; call me when you're ready for me to cook."

• Changing Approach Isn't Easy •

One afternoon I walked in from work and found dishes on the kitchen table and sweaters, schoolbooks, and toys spread about the house. There was a sofa full of clean laundry waiting to be folded and three kids deep in a Monopoly game.

All my learning vanished! "Look at this mess—what do you think you're doing? No one's done their chores! I'm late, tired, and this house is a pig pen! Who was supposed to fold clothes, pick up, do the kitchen?" Hands on my hips, I stood there, the formidable sergeant. "All of you, move!"

Barbara, 12 years old and mouthy, tossed her head and muttered as she passed, "Thought we were learning some new ways of communicating around here. Sure sounds like the old mother to me!"

I wanted to answer in kind, but from somewhere I remembered hearing: *When all else fails and you're under full attack, try being honest!* "We are, but apparently I don't know enough yet!" I still sounded angry, but it was the best I could do. "I'll change my clothes and be down in fifteen minutes."

When I returned, Barbara and Teresa were voluntarily working together getting the kitchen into shape and dinner underway. "You sounded so hungry and tired," the "mouthy" one began. "We've made a salad, and frozen pizza's in the oven!" Whee! Maybe they didn't need me doing it right for them to understand. I was encouraged.

The next day I was given a second chance. Upon opening the door, I again found dirty dishes everywhere and flour on the floor. Yet this time I felt different. *I could choose to react differently.* I moved close to Teresa, touched her hair, and said, "I smell a pie cooking and I feel like a kid waiting for dessert!"

She grinned, "Yeah, and it's a mess in here, but we've made three pies! Go on upstairs, the kitchen will be clean when you come down."

Pure gold, and I hadn't even mentioned the kitchen or the eight-year-old playing with dough!

Upstairs, another hurdle. Matt's room had been such a disaster that at seven in the morning I'd put "clean up" on his work list with exclamation marks and a big "TODAY!"

"Remember," I said to myself, "*note any small, real improvement, describe it, and react with your feelings in an 'I' statement.*" Nothing had been done, but with my new eyes the words came. Rumpling his hair, I said, "When I see you at your desk with textbook open and pen in hand, you must know my heart leaps with joy."

Grinning sheepishly, he said, "I forgot my part of a team assignment. If I finish it now it can still be put in the school computer. Don't worry, I'll do my room tonight."

What was happening? I wasn't being a complaining, fault-finding mother, but neither was I giving undeserved praise. I was simply being a reasonable adult reacting in a truthful, loving manner to my children, and they were responding in kind.

• Compromise Between Parent and Child •

Did Matt's bedroom meet my expectations later? No, and truthfully, it never did unless I joined him in the cleaning (which incidentally is not a bad way to handle chores periodically). However, there was some improvement. I described the changes and shared my feelings of pleasure at his keeping his promise about working on the room before sleeping.

Still, I was spending too much time on his room situation. Neither Clif nor I could say, "Just close your door and don't let us see it." We were not fanatical about cleanliness, but we were simply not capable of turning a part of our house over to a kid to do with totally as he pleased.

On the weekend, I met with Matt. After describing the situation and my feelings, I wondered if there were any way we could find a common meeting ground for our conflicting ideas of cleanliness.

Astutely, he answered, "I don't know, Mom. What is absolutely mandatory for your daily peace of mind?"

Magically, those words became part of our family problem-solving terminology. They were a fine starting point for talking over touchy matters. Some things were just annoyances. Some were worse, and maybe, just one thing was so distressing or disruptive it had to be resolved to ensure peace of mind.

With what level of disorder could I live? With what degree of cleanliness could Matt? Maybe our conflict wasn't just about chores!

• Handling Peer Problems Positively •

Parents tend to blame adolescent difficulties on those people with whom a child chooses to associate. For years we've encouraged our children's participation in positive, supervised activities. Now, suddenly, the fun our adolescent shares with friends is often unsupervised or involves behavior that conflicts with our values, the law, or our child's health and safety.

However, this nationwide, rapid increase in unacceptable adolescent behavior has not happened because of peer pressure. Our children's world is the result of decades of social, economic, and cultural changes that have influenced our laws and institutions as well as adult values, authority, and adolescent behavior. None of us can ignore the hours of media material that graphically demonstrates to us and our children the glamour and excitement of unrestricted adult behavior and the ease of moving into it.

Still, adolescent peer pressure is real. As adults we encourage our friends to participate in the activities we enjoy. Our children and their friends do the same, with an adolescent often doing with another teen what he wouldn't do alone. Sharing a forbidden behavior makes that behavior seem more acceptable and brings all participants friendship, closeness, and group approval.

For several months one of our daughters had been increasingly involved with a group we felt was moving her too rapidly into activities not befitting her age or our values. Her new best friend, Melissa (not her real name), seemed daily to find ways of challenging our standards and home routines.

Instead of riding the school bus, our daughter was now given rides by Melissa, who had her own car. I heard about their after-school activities and about shoplifting and subsequent police apprehension of one of our daughter's new friends. Our daughter even told me of her own concerns when Melissa went to her boyfriend's home for lunch while his parents were at work.

I tried not to be critical, but I couldn't miss the smell of smoke on Melissa's clothes or her rebellious language toward those in authority. Often I found myself reacting negatively to a whispered conversation, a sudden change of plans, or Melissa's telephone lies to her parents.

Soon my tight jaw, rigid back, and disapproving looks also expressed my growing concern and unhappiness. Alone with our daughter, my judgmental comments were becoming more direct. I didn't like Melissa and I believed she and her friends were having a negative influence on our daughter's behavior.

Finally, when one more problem-solving session with my daughter turned into a parental lecture filled with my fears and concerns, she slammed out of the house, declaring, "I'm not going to listen to you talk about my friends ever again! If you don't like Melissa that's your problem. She's my friend! They're all my friends, and I like being with them better than anyone else in the world. And stop blaming Melissa for my behavior. I'm doing what I want to do!"

• Changing Your Feelings Will Change Your Attitude •

Our daughter was right. Already she was choosing to be with her friends elsewhere, whenever possible, and to give us only the most necessary information about their activities. Yet, as the adult, wasn't I supposed to react negatively to negative situations and out-of-line behavior?

Yes, but not in the manner I was doing. Regularly I expressed my displeasure with looks of disapproval and words of criticism, blame, or judgment. It was as if those were the only tools I had for influencing her behavior. I was repeating what I'd done with our children and their chores.

———

The philosopher Marcus Aurelius wrote:
If you are distressed by something external, the pain is not due to the thing itself, but to your own estimate of it. This you have the power to revoke at any minute.

For weeks, I'd had those words taped to my mirror. Now in a flash, they came to my mind and freed me from my fault-finding, fear-filled position. Our daughter and her friends knew our values, concerns, and feelings about everything they were doing. My judgmental attitude was accomplishing nothing. I didn't need to be angry and upset over their adolescent behavior to talk with them about it.

For longer than I liked to remember, I'd apparently felt it my responsibility, as a parent, to feel disappointed, hurt, or unhappy when our children were not living up to our expectations. Then deliberately, I'd reflect my feelings to them so they would stop, change, or be sorry. Since this behavior worked when they were small, it seemed natural as they became older and their problems more serious for my feelings of fear, pain, disappointment, or disapproval to be more pronounced.

Only now my feelings and words didn't affect their adolescent behavior. Then, the children's problems were minor and our involvement in their lives was desired and necessary. Now, my feelings were hindering my ability to participate in our daughter's life. If we were not there for her in a way that encouraged rather than discouraged sharing, with whom but her peers would she discuss important experiences?

• Change Your Behavior •

We parents walk a fine line between help and hindrance when we deal with our adolescent and his friends, but the effort to interact and communicate is worthwhile. The friends our child gathers around him are a reflection of his own life, needs, and choices. When we criticize his friends, we criticize him. We either become partners with our adolescent in his process of growth, or we become his enemy, fighting daily battles about our differences.

Parents have nothing to gain and everything to lose when they get into battles with their children about their friends. Your influence with your youngster is greatest when you, your child, and his friends are able to communicate about common goals in a cooperative problem-solving way.

With our daughter and Melissa, such a partnership required that I change my attitude from one of criticism and judgment to one of genuine listening to *their* viewpoint and considering *their* interests. Marcus Aurelius's words of wisdom helped with my attitude. My decision to treat Melissa as if she were *already* the friend I wanted her to become to our daughter gave me directions for changing my behavior.

If an adolescent is already the kind of friend you want for your child, then you'll react positively towards that person and under no circumstances will you make derogatory comments about her to anyone.

I told my daughter that she was right. I'd been overreacting and I'd like another chance to get to know her group. This simple shift of attitude relaxed my reaction to all of the group. I greeted them with smiles and listened more. I watched for the little things that were positive and unique in their lives and personalities and used the three-part sentence to note them. I asked questions that required them to think (not simple yes or no questions) and listened to their responses without giving advice or my opinion. As my feelings, words, and behavior changed, so did theirs.

One day, while waiting for our daughter to get home from her part-time job, Melissa joined me in the kitchen and brought up a personal situation that was troubling her. In two quick sentences she told me about the problem and wondered how I'd handle it if I were in her place.

I knew what she needed and now I could provide it. "That's a tough one," I said, sitting down at the table and reaching for her hand. "You must have all kinds of thoughts going around in your mind about this. Tell me what you've been thinking." And she did, in great detail and with a growing awareness of the choices she could make and the consequences each might bring into her life. She was finding her own answer.

As we grow, so do our children and their friends.

———

Sometime later, our daughter burst into the house, full of excitement and talk about going to her first rock concert. "It's in San Francisco, Mom, and there'll be six of us going. Melissa's boyfriend will drive his car. I can go, can't I?" I wanted to say "no," but that would have been in keeping with my old fears and feelings. Now, I needed to tell her through my behavior and attitude that we would make this decision together.

"Let's see if we can make it okay. I've never been to a rock concert, but maybe you and Melissa can talk to your friends and their older brothers and sisters. Get their ideas of what you might expect on anything and everything and their suggestions for handling problems. I'll talk to some of my parent friends and get their input. We'll get back together, pool our knowledge, and see if we can make this work."

Peer pressure and a desire to conform to the group can work positively as well as negatively. I'll never forget the information the concert group gathered. It was much more relevant than anything my parent friends had to offer. The teens' planning, problem solving, and their successful experience demonstrated the creativity that adolescents develop when criticism is absent and they know everyone is working towards peace-of-mind goals. Take time to get acquainted with your children's friends. If you're lucky, they may become your friends, too.

As we walk the fine line of balancing parental responsibilities with adolescent needs for freedom and independence, we're doing exactly what we're supposed to be doing: Holding the fort while at the same time loosening the tie that binds.

• The Absence of Criticism •

It is difficult to reduce the negatives we use with our adolescent children unless we regularly re-examine our attitude towards their behavior. We can't avoid the challenges teenagers bring into our lives, but we can change the way we handle them.

Refraining from criticism and recognizing our children's strengths are powerful tonics for family relationships. Practicing both can break down walls of inadequacy and free our children's natural motivation and creativity.

Changing Our Attitudes

• Steps to Change •

Examine your position on adolescent problems. Do you find yourself relying on criticism, anger, and punishment to get results? Continually high expectations and regular criticism are not conducive to the rearing of self-motivated children.

Develop a new attitude. Understand that how you think about an adolescent's behavior determines your feelings and your reactions to it. This you can change.

Commit to a more positive approach on first contact with your teenager. Look for the smallest part of the child's effort that you can appreciate. Use the three-step sentence to describe what you see, how it makes you feel, and why.

Create a more relaxed home climate. React with humor, tolerance, and honesty. Get in the habit of seeing and noting small improvements immediately. Delay asking for further effort.

Become a partner with your adolescent in his growth experience. Seek solutions you and your adolescent can both view positively and handle successfully. Commit to a relationship-building approach.

7

Love in Action

New Belief: *Our expectations for a situation color and define our experience of it.*

• Unfulfilled Expectations •

I can still hear our daughter, in a moment of disagreement, saying to me about her older brother, "You don't love me like you do him!"

Then instantly, my retort, "How can you say that when you both need braces and you're getting them and he isn't?"

"But you never spend time with just me!"

"What about last Saturday? Shopping for four hours and lunch out, isn't that time?"

My responses were full of truth, but that was the trouble. She wasn't talking about facts. She was talking about feelings! Do braces feel like love when she hears, "Don't crunch ice, or chew gum, or bite that apple," when braces have wires that come loose and bands that need tightening and every trip to the orthodontist means an hour of waiting for a two-minute adjustment?

As for the shopping, she wants brand-name clothes. I want the ones on sale. She's tall, thin, and not yet mature enough to move from preteen to junior-size clothes. As we search, hourly she hears, "You're too long here" or "too small there."

Finally, exhausted, we seek the respite of lunch. She wants to go to the place her best friend's mother takes her; I know their prices and I'd like McDonald's. She'd starve first. We settle for an in-between that's crowded and offers neither atmosphere nor economy.

Still, we're sitting down comfortably, and we begin to relax. Then we each realize we have a captive audience of one, at the mercy of whatever concern she chooses to raise.

"I forgot to tell you, Mom, but I have to have a new bathing suit. The seat's worn through in my old one."

Oh, no! If dresses and shoes are difficult, a bathing suit's impossible.

Then it's my turn, concerning a phone conversation I've overheard: "You're not really planning to have your friend visit while you're baby-sitting, are you?" Or maybe it's the continuation of an earlier problem, "We need to talk further about your after-school stops at the store. Your father and I . . . "

For my daughter, the shopping day had been one surge of pain after another. We'd argued over clothes, their cost, and her behavior. She'd come home knowing she ought to feel loving and grateful, but she didn't. Her mind was on her changed baby-sitting plans; the new jeans that looked like brand-name jeans, but weren't; and the possibility of stuffing her bra with cotton.

On the other hand, I'd given her a day of my time and attention and had spent more money than I could afford. I felt entitled to a guarantee of cooperation. After all, we'd even found her a fairly satisfactory bathing suit!

We're home and her sister's late getting in, so I suggest she set the table and make the salad. She jumps up, shouting, "Why? I always do her work, she gets all the fun! All I do is work, work, work!"

"How can you say that?" I retort angrily. "We've been doing things for you all day! Don't you appreciate anything?"

• The Feelings Called Love •

Love is an interesting concept. It covers so much territory. Webster says it's a strong attachment, affection, or devotion to something or someone. We love our pets, our car, a movie, a television star. We love peach ice cream, sunny days, this person today and that one tomorrow.

Everyone's idea of love is different. I hardly understand the uses of the word anymore. I've seen terrible, often life-long, emotional and physical damage caused by someone's action in the name of "love." We all read the papers and see the atrocities of terrorism and war justified by love of country or religion.

I'd thought of love and its definitions occasionally, but not deeply. Then our 8-year-old daughter came home full of excitement about a father-daughter banquet her Blue Bird troop leader had planned for their group. She asked Clif if he'd go with her, and he agreed to think about it.

He thought, then he came to me, deeply entrenched in his position: "No, I'm not going on any such outing ever. I can't think of anything worse for me than ten grown men, who don't know each other and have nothing in common but Blue Bird daughters, getting together for two hours and pretending they're having fun with an equal number of giggly, nervous little girls."

In the days that followed, nothing Teresa or I said changed his mind. Finally, in anger and tears she declared, "All the other fathers are going. If you really loved me, you'd go!"

I looked at Clif. Surely now he would relent. Instead, he just touched her face gently, and said, "I'm sorry about the dinner, but I don't think you really doubt my love for you. Think about it."

That evening I noticed her nestling against his shoulder, happily writing her spelling words as he dictated them. They seemed on good terms, but how could they be? I was still upset over his unreasonable position. En route to bed, Teresa whispered in my ear, "Tell Daddy to show you the letter I wrote to him."

In her letter, she'd written: "I do know you love me. You taught me to swim, ride a bicycle, and skate. You play Monopoly and Hearts with us. You take us to cut Christmas trees. You come to get me when I fall. You won't let big kids fight me. You work for us. You help me with schoolwork. You made us the climbing gym and fort. You play croquet with us. You like having me help you in the yard. You think I'm pretty."

The things Clif did with Teresa made her feel safe, capable, and treasured. He was there when she needed him. He gave her his time, support, and attention on things they both enjoyed. What he didn't do was deliberately suffer in the name of love for children unless crucial circumstances warranted it.

I also noticed that almost everything on her list involved an interaction with her father through some kind of activity. And, why not? From the day our children are born we show them our love through what we do with them and how we do it. Showing love is easy when they're young and their world is the one we choose to establish for them. We know their needs, and we can supply them. We know their desires and can accommodate them. We plan an activity that is age and ability appropriate and everything works out great.

As the children grow older, doing things together becomes more difficult. Their likes and needs are now created from a complex blend of adolescent growth, family influence, and outside, ever-changing people, choices, and experiences. Their idea of what constitutes a meaningful activity may change from one moment to the next.

• Examining Plans and Expectations •

Considering the love and effort we put into the activities we do for our maturing children, it behooves us to consider carefully what makes these activities successful or unsuccessful.

Clif and I talked of other situations entered into with love and high expectations that ended in deep dissatisfaction for everyone. As most parents know, unhappiness may begin with one person, but it quickly spreads to all participants. Using hindsight, we recognized one of our difficulties was in trying to get too much from an individual situation.

It wasn't wrong for me, with six children, to see any private time with a child as a time to express love for the youngster *and* a time to do some one-to-one problem solving with her. Neither was it out of line for our daughter to want all her emotional and material needs to be met on a special day reserved just for her. However, combining of emotional and practical needs is seldom effective.

Also, most parents at times agree to an overly expensive or undesirable situation with the unstated, and perhaps unrealistic, expectation that the youngster's later appreciation and cooperation will compensate for their all-out parental effort. Such conflict in goals particularly arises when the request comes under the stress of what is presented as an immediate need. Short notice creates an emotional climate not conducive to parent or child satisfaction.

Until now, Clif and I had operated under a "parents know best" attitude towards activities involving our participation. Yet more and more often, as with the shopping trip for our teenage daughter, things didn't work out the way we thought they would. Clif and I were ready to change our attitude and our behavior.

We wanted to make parent-child planning for activities a shared priority. We wanted to consider, in advance, the short- and long-term importance the activity held in the child's life and in ours; what must be accomplished for the event to be successful and what was optional. We wanted to talk about preparation, behavior, costs, and who was responsible for what. We expected some of the planning time to be focused on the safety, health, and personal limitations of all involved parties.

Out of such thoughts came a new rule developed for the benefit of parents: *A planning session will occur prior to any activity involving parental permission, participation, or cooperation.*

• Planning Implementation •

Recognize the purpose. Planning sessions are for communicating desires, needs, feelings, and thoughts. They are for talking of goals, risks, and responsibilities. They are for considering the youngster's contributions to an activity as well as the parent's. In other words, they are sessions where parent and child share in the decisions and the responsibility that make activities successful— physically and emotionally.

Establish a pattern. A telephone call comes through with an invitation and the child wants an answer while her friend holds the line. Even though she knows you are following your new plan, she's indignant at your insistence that she hang up and call her friend back after you've talked. Establishing planning as a fact of life will be awkward at first, and neither your children nor their friends will like it. Remember, they do not need to like it.

Our goal is to change an approach that hasn't been working. However, people generally resist change. A child's not liking change does not mean change is wrong. We don't even have to defend our idea, just hear their feelings and restate our plan.

"I know advance planning seems a cumbersome process and a real inconvenience to your friend and you. You both want answers right now, but we're not operating that way anymore. I'll meet you in the den right after dinner and we'll talk then."

Ah, what a good feeling inside of me. Our dinner time did not have to be spent on problem solving. We weren't chained to a telephone bell and the children's requests for instant permission, transportation, and help. They adjusted fast. Within days, advance planning was considered standard operating procedure in our household.

Insist on privacy. The purpose of the planning session is defeated when friends, relatives, store clerks, coaches, or dates are unnecessarily involved. The requests your children make in the presence of others deserve the same treatment as those made with someone waiting on the telephone. That is, "We'll need to talk about this and then my youngster will get back to you."

Make lists. There's something very satisfying in leaving a planning session with thoughts in writing. I recall spontaneously suggesting a day at the county fair for myself, a visiting friend, and our combined youngsters. I didn't know about formal planning sessions then. The children were all between seven and ten years of age and we should have had a great time. Instead, everything went wrong!

We had not preplanned money, food, activities, safety rules, or length of stay. We'd not discussed goals. Conflicts arose at every suggestion anyone made and within an hour my friend and I regretted spending the day at the fair.

• The Planning Session Pay-Off •

During a later summer with several preteen and early adolescent youngsters visiting us, a day on the coast seemed a good idea. By this time, I had learned my lesson.

The planning session began with a discussion of the choices available. After all, the day was for the children and I wanted to get points for my efforts. I was sure they'd want the beach with the boardwalk, rides, and food concessions. Not so; with only a minimum of discussion, the visiting children convinced ours the more deserted beach with picnic food and wave-riding equipment would be more fun.

We talked of likes, limitations, and difficulties. We discussed food preferences, types of beach equipment available, and money. We considered sunburn prevention, hot sand, facilities at this beach, and extra clothing needs. We discussed travel time, behavior in the car, transporting supplies from the car to the water's edge, and beach safety.

I wrote down the main things they wanted from the day and any less important items that came up. As we talked, I realized again my tendency to schedule too much in a day. Several times I had to consciously resist including other ideas.

When the fog came in and the weather turned cold, we had extra clothing and a list of maybe's that included a tour of an old World War I concrete boat grounded near shore, now serving as a fishing pier far into the ocean. I'd forgotten how fascinating sea gulls diving for food and weathered old men pulling in their nets and lines could be.

In days of old, I'd have thought I had to compensate for the bad weather with time on the boardwalk. That time would have doubled my planned budget, overtaxed my energy, and ended up being too little for the kids and too much for me. Instead, we had the easiest trip to the beach I'd ever taken with the children, and they declared it the high spot of their summer.

The more our children consider their desires and how they can be met, the more successful they'll be in achieving them.

• Responsibility Shared/Satisfaction Guaranteed •

Once started, the planning process seems to move with its own momentum. A request or need will be brought to your attention and rather than immediately thinking, "Is this right or wrong, dangerous or safe, extravagant or manageable?" your first thoughts will be of a planning session.

Soon the negative and difficult aspects of a situation are not reasons for parental nonparticipation or denial of a request. They are just parts of the picture that need problem solving so all participants can be reasonably assured of a successful activity.

You'll be doing in your planning sessions what most adults do routinely in life with their problems:

- Discuss short- and long-term goals.
- Consider expectations and options.
- Talk about limitations, difficulties, and contributions.
- Recognize ownership and establish responsibility.
- Brainstorm solutions to problems.

- Talk of the best and worst that could happen.
- Compare advantages and risks.
- Seek more information.
- Take notes, make lists, and review individual responsibility.

Involving children in a process that requires all participants to respect and consider differing attitudes, feelings, concerns, goals, and limitations in order to get their own needs and desires met is reality-based problem solving.

• On-the-Job Satisfaction •

Very quickly Clif and I began to feel a sense of rationality and order in our lives. We were still talking, planning, and problem solving with our kids, but the atmosphere was different. Time had become our friend. We were no longer on a roller coaster of preteen and adolescent demands and frustrations.

Other good things were happening, too. A few months into our practicing this policy, one of the youngsters commented on how little we were worrying about him, "Is it because I'm older and in middle school?" he asked.

Certainly our planning sessions were making us more at ease with the idea of openly defining who owned a problem. With every reminder our children stuck to their backpacks, placed on the refrigerator, or put on the car steering wheel, we were gaining confidence in their abilities to be responsible for their own lives. Every time we saw them handle their own forgotten dental appointment or anticipate our concerns in advance with collected information, we became more willing to let them take risks, make choices, and experience consequences. In other words, as they grew, we grew.

• Planning the Use of Family Money •

Problems with money are thought provoking and deserve much attention. Shopping trips provide great opportunities for practice in planning how to spend money. Needs for clothing and possessions change with a child's age, interests, and body shape. The media influences their desires with advertising and their peers do it with social pressure. The results of these myriad pressures test our patience, finances, values, flexibility, and communication skills.

Some of us eventually decide to give up on the situation and put the child on a monthly or yearly shopping allowance. We often add, "The money is in your hands. You shop, you decide, you find out how far the money goes. It's your problem."

Really? Will you honestly allow her to buy any dress, sweater, or bathing suit she wants? Can he say, "Good, I don't need new clothes. I'll use the money on a wet-suit or a new surfboard." If not, when will you disapprove—after the item has been bought and brought home?

Are you going to keep tabs on each new item your youngsters buy and then total their monthly or yearly purchases? Probably not, since that would defeat the purpose of the clothes allowance. Yet, if you're never involved in shopping for a purchase, how will you know the price of children's clothes and whether new items came from a sale or a shoplifting experience?

Shopping trips, and the decisions surrounding them, force parent-child communication on situations of vital importance to children. Their spending of our money requires joint participation in planning sessions.

• Money the Child Earns •

Today, our children with summer and after-school jobs can earn enough money to purchase their own telephones and televisions, buy cars and motorcycles, go to Europe for three months, or support a drug habit.

Often a parent hears from a child, "It's my money, I've earned it. Why should you tell me how to spend it?" After experiencing several such "my money" conflicts, Clif and I called for a problem-solving session to decide our rights in regard to the money our youngsters earned.

During the discussion, it quickly became apparent that Clif and I were always planning ahead for expenditures that directly benefitted our children and only indirectly us. With the hope that each would go to college, our plans could continue into their adult years. Since it was our money that took care of their basic needs and made it possible for them to use their money for other things, we felt we had a right to be involved in how some of their money was spent.

As a trial solution, it was decided that half of everything these older children earned would go into a separate savings account that could be used only for major purchases, college, or travel. This fund would require our agreement on its use so long as they were our dependents or were anticipating future financial help from us.

• The Importance of Planning Increases as Children Grow •

Ginny had $3,000 in her special savings account by the end of her senior year in high school and could afford to go to Europe. She knew our concerns would need consideration.

While we were in favor of the trip and the experiences it would offer her, $3,000 was still a lot of money at our house. So we began, "When we think of you taking all your savings for this trip to Europe we find ourselves becoming really uncomfortable. You don't seem very sure about your plans. You talk of getting a job in Europe, but you do not know how, where, or even if you can be a tourist and also work. It seems you could return home in September without money or plans."

She nodded and then brought up specifically the things troubling us. She talked of her present, casual interest in making good grades, her extremely active social life, and more important, her lack of career direction. "Maybe I need a break from school. Would you feel better if I were definitely planning to postpone college for a year? I could work and save again for college."

We liked the idea very much; and also her willingness to leave $500 in her checking account for emergencies or immediate expenses after her return from Europe.

As our children move into adulthood, our input into their decisions lessens. This is as it should be. Nevertheless, our financial or physical participation in their solutions may continue to occur.

With this in mind, everything we can learn about communicating our position and taking care of our own needs is helpful. Planning sessions encourage family communication and closeness. They also prevent the deep regrets many parents have with those second thoughts that come after they've said yes.

Developed for parents, advance planning sessions benefit everyone. Where power, responsibility, and decisions are shared, feelings of love can flow unhindered.

Love in Action

• Steps to Change •

Recognize love in action. Evaluate your success with family activities undertaken for the direct benefit of your children. If better planning could have changed the outcome, change your approach.

Make a planning-session rule. Your aim is to discuss with your child, in advance, all situations requiring your permission or participation.

Establish a pattern of privacy. Do not consider a request while a third person holds on the telephone or is personally present.

Follow good problem-solving procedures in the session. Establish goals, consider expectations and problems. Share planning, decisions, and responsibility for making the activity successful.

Develop a life-long commitment to advance planning. Your participation in your youngster's life will continue throughout your life. Be diligent about getting your own needs heard and met.

8

School Problems

New Belief: *When we react to our children's school problems as if they were ours, we interfere with our children's ability to experience them as theirs.*

• Recognizing Parental Overreaction •

Parents sometimes get messages from a middle or junior-high school staff member that indicate unexpected or dramatic dissatisfaction with some aspect of a youngster's behavior. Suddenly, we want to grab our child and scream! We're filled with overwhelming anger and we want the child to feel as bad as we do. We're overreacting.

———

One day, Matt walked in and handed me an envelope from his vice principal. Inside was a referral slip stating he'd made a vulgar hand sign at a school-bus driver!

Did I own the problem? It sure felt like it. I was furious! How could he do this? How dare he do it! My anger was consuming. "I can't believe this! Go to the backyard. Now!" I yelled.

He started to answer, and my hand went up. "Stop. Don't try to explain. If you say a word, I don't know what I'll do!" He understood and left. Wisely so. He was our fifth child and, despite my experience, here I was, full of rage and ready for battle.

It was all right for him to see my anger, but I knew I didn't dare deal with him emotionally or physically in that condition. Anything I did or said would be too much. I had to take time out.

Once he was out of my presence, I was able to ask myself some questions about my inappropriate, overpowering anger:

- Why was I feeling so strongly about this situation?
- What other emotions did I feel besides anger?
- When had such a situation arisen before in my life?
- What did it mean to me then?

I took time to listen to my answers, think about the emotions surrounding them, and recognize the first feelings of embarrassment and hurt that were there for just a flash before the inappropriate one of intense anger (my second, cover-up feeling) took over. Such thought was an effective way to get insight into my immediate emotion and the old facts and feelings that had shaped it.

Later, when I called Matt in, he immediately questioned my anger. "Why were you so mad? I knew you'd be upset, but not like that. It wasn't the worst thing I could have done."

"I know, but at that moment it was to me." Then I explained what I'd found when I'd asked myself the same question. "When I was your age, it was more than a sign of disrespect. It was something only the worst, toughest kid in school would have done, and he'd have been instantly expelled from school for doing it."

• Calm Response Improves Communication •

I was surprised at how calm and collected I was feeling, how easily I was able to talk about the situation. Then I realized: *This calmness was my key to knowing I'd found my hidden emotions.* In identifying the background of experience I had tied to his behavior, I could again feel the embarrassment and hurt I'd so instantly hid beneath my overreacting anger. I was still feeling strong emotions, but my reaction was different. Now I could discuss them rationally.

"With all those old facts and feelings, imagine me hearing my son has done this and his vice principal, who I see at county meetings every month, knows." With a wry grin, I added, "Don't you know counselors' children aren't supposed to do such things?"

"Yeah, but, Mom, the bus driver put me off the bus for a week for something I didn't do! I laughed, but I didn't throw the kid's lunch. The driver wouldn't listen, just wrote out a referral. Yesterday as I was walking home she honked her horn so I'd turn and look at her. Then she just smiled and nodded as she drove past me."

I paraphrased what he'd said, guessed at his feelings, listened as he told me more of the bus driver's general lack of skill in detecting troublemakers, and then moved directly back to the problem.

"But to make the finger sign at a woman! I know kids do it among themselves, but it's such a degrading, vulgar thing to do to someone. I hate it. Do you know what it really means?"

"Mommm. Of course I do, but kids don't think about that. No one does. Anyway, I'm not a tough kid. I'm not like those you were talking about." His eyes held mine. "You know that, don't you?"

Suddenly, peace filled my heart. My out-of-proportion feelings were connected to former beliefs, not present facts. I nodded slowly, "Yes, I do know." Then my hand touched his arm. "But what about this notice? The vice principal was angry enough to send it in an envelope addressed to me. I have to respond."

He was quiet for a moment, then slowly he answered, "He was upset, but not like you were. What if I write on the note that you and I have talked, that I'm sorry I did it, and I'll apologize to the driver in his office. Maybe that's all he wants, just to know I'm sorry I did it and that it won't happen again. We could both sign the note." Suddenly, he looked up. "Mom, you know, don't you, I didn't think about it meaning so much to you . . . or the bus driver?"

I smiled and nodded. Yes, I did know.

• When to Get Professional Help •

Sometimes the behavior of our children is so shockingly contrary to our basic beliefs, or touches on such deeply hidden feelings, that we can't hold back our words of judgment and anger. Before we can stop, our feelings pour out in a flood of hostile, hurtful statements.

The devastation takes it toll. She runs to her bedroom and stays there sobbing. He stomps out of the house, furious and defeated, vowing he's never going back to school. We feel terrible.

How could we say all those awful things? Then we think again of their behavior and we burn. Our anger returns. We want to go back and punish the child more. We want him to feel the pain we're feeling.

These negative reactions happen to all of us at some time with someone we love. Even when we've identified a hidden feeling once, we may not be able to prevent our old emotions, values, and the mental pictures we hold of ourselves, our children, and others we love from surfacing again.

A skilled, nonjudgmental listener can help us identify patterns and hidden emotions. In my lifetime, I've been blessed with attentive friends, caring mentors, and sympathetic fellow workers who were there when I needed them. I have also sought professional counseling.

We aren't superhuman beings. We're everyday people, strong in some situations, weak in others. We do our best with what we have. When the unbearable pain is in our foot, we go to a foot doctor. When an ongoing, inappropriate reaction tells us there's pain in our emotional circuit, the wise person goes to a counselor.

• The Lasting Impact of Negative Messages •

Problems will be with us always. We cannot physically stop our children from cutting school, misbehaving, failing, using drugs, or having sex. That's not the whole story, however. Our children do know our values. Since babyhood they've heard us say: "Don't spit, bite, hit, steal, cheat, deface or hammer on walls. Don't cut school, lie, be rude to teachers, or bully others. Be kind, share, listen, respect rules and those in authority. Stay away from drugs, sex, and the wrong crowd." They know what we hold in our hearts as valuable for their behavior and growth.

This is equally true even if your youngster has a history of behavior problems. You've surely said all your best lines before. Now, silence them and choose hope as your feeling. Begin to think of your child as capable of changing her ways. Verbalize your belief in her ability to take the responsibility for the consequences of her behavior and learn from them.

While adult reaction may tell you of the seriousness of a situation in the eyes of school or community authorities, this does not mean your child has done something from which she will never recover.

Adolescents do all kinds of things we never would have believed they'd do, and these same young people still become law-abiding, gainfully employed, tender-hearted wives, husbands, and parents.

All teenagers may not become everything we would like them to be, but the majority of these young people, and their friends, grow up into self-sufficient, contributing adults, getting along reasonably well with their parents and making our world better. This number even includes those we are sure are a bad influence on our children and will never amount to much anyway!

Accusations and dire predictions from those who know and love us best carry tremendous weight. Negative words from an angry parent can bounce around in our minds for years, detracting from our successes and adding to the pain of our failures.

Our children's behavior may be horrible. It may affect their grades, graduation, or happiness. However, we do more harm than good to verbalize the belief that a child's behavior will result in her failure in school, becoming a juvenile delinquent or drug addict, or missing out on chances for jobs, college, and the better things in life.

When our words carry high levels of anger, disappointment, and disapproval, we're being affected by our child's behavior and its consequences as if the bad things were happening to us. Try not to voice such feelings. Our child's school behavior, and the experiences that follow it, belong physically and emotionally to her.

Let's assume now you've looked at your own feelings and have made, at least, temporary peace with them. You are again in touch with your desire to have your response to school situations honor the new relationship you're building with your child and are prepared to communicate calmly, knowing the problem is not something that has personally happened to you.

• How to Communicate Calmly •

Describe the situation. "I just received a phone call from your principal. He said you were throwing lighted firecrackers and smoke bombs on the school grounds."

Express your feelings. "He told me of the injuries this behavior has caused at other schools. We're both concerned about the seriousness of this."

State next action. "You and I are to meet with him in his office tomorrow morning."

Do not mention school discipline at this time even if the principal specifically discussed these measures. You may want to, but think a moment. How would you want your spouse to react if you'd just backed your new car into a tree? You'd want to have a chance to explain how it happened and express your regrets, fears, and feelings.

If you can give your child this courtesy as he claims the school's not fair, that others did it too and didn't get caught, you'll be listening with your heart. You need only reply with the truth, "It's hard to be the one caught." Remember, you're being his friend, listening to his words, and understanding his feelings.

Your caring acknowledgment of his feelings does not mean you are excusing his behavior. The school has judged his behavior and found him guilty. Your youngster does not need more judgment from you. He knows you do not condone breaking rules and taking unnecessary risks. Your calm sharing of the school's concern and your later acceptance of the consequences for your child's actions clearly indicate your responsible, adult position.

• Preparing for School Conferences •

It is your youngster's behavior under discussion, so he should be present for any school conferences about his behavior. It's helpful if he understands the school meeting is not to focus on extraneous circumstances that may have contributed to the behavior (i.e., "so and so did it too"). Community and school rules are made for the safety and education of many. They are rules of life our children need to learn.

Most school personnel are professionally trained educators and use proven methods in their teaching and discipline. If we want them to assume the major responsibility for the education of our children, they must also have our support of their authority. The opportunities for growth their supervision offers to our children are unlimited.

With that philosophy in mind, we'll not want to undermine or dilute the teacher's effectiveness. Remember in Chapter 3 when Clif and I identified our family problems, assigned ownership, and divided responsibility? It is healthy for the same to occur with the problems our children experience in school.

Our children know where our soft spots are. They are as skillful at sending arrows to those sensitive areas in a teacher/parent conference as they are at home. You're not present at the conference to solve the problems for them.

• Effective Participation in School Conferences •

Establish a communicative atmosphere. Express your appreciation to the staff member for his concern and acknowledge you share it. Ask the teacher to summarize for you and your youngster the problem so all three of you will be working from the same base.

Check your youngster's understanding of the situation. When the adult finishes, ask your child to *rephrase the teacher's presentation of the problem* in his own words. This includes identifying his own problem behavior and its consequences in grades, the classroom environment, or the teacher's feelings.

Create speaking time for your youngster. Face your child and convey your desire to hear his ideas and feelings. Perhaps say, "You seem to understand the situation and your teacher's concerns. Do you want to add anything from your viewpoint and feelings?"

Ensure adult acknowledgment or response. If the teacher does not react, it is always suitable for a parent to ask for more information or clarification from the youngster. "Are you saying you speak out because you think your teacher doesn't really understand the situation?"

Listen to the teen's reply, restate it in your own words, and go back to the problem. "Still, with thirty students and only one teacher, it's thirty-to-one and your teacher says that's not manageable for her. She wants your concerns handled some other way. You've been giving this thought. Perhaps you have an idea on how this can be resolved satisfactorily for you both?"

Now, the conference is really between the student and the educator. You have established a communication base for problem solving. Your child has choices to make and the teacher has more consequences she can use.

• Homework in Middle School •

Every spring, most middle schools hold orientation programs for incoming students and their parents. At such gatherings, staff members discuss school rules, expectations, and the difficulties some students experience in changing schedules, classrooms, teachers, and peers. They talk about school activities, the availability of counselors and staff for assistance in problems, and the importance of home and school communication.

Finally, a speaker addresses the subject of homework and his belief that a student's commitment to doing the required school assignments on a daily basis is the single most important factor in school success.

You give your child a serious look and nod in agreement. The speaker continues: "Getting behind in homework affects many aspects of a youngster's life—not just grades, but test scores, classroom participation, social behavior, and self-confidence."

Now you're really worried. You know your child has taken homework too casually, doing some well, some half-heartedly, and some not at all. Her teachers and you have talked often in your efforts to get this capable child to perform according to her ability.

You nudge her and whisper: "Did you hear that? Isn't it what I've been telling you? Middle school's a whole new ball game. You'll fail here if you don't do the work. You've got to get serious about your studying. You're going to do your homework every night and I'm going to check it."

Don't say what you're thinking, and if you did, backtrack at the next opportunity!

What the speaker believes about homework may be true, but what you've been doing to get your child to do her homework hasn't been working. You're reading this book to consider a more effective way. Don't go back to using power and control.

You want your *child* to be responsible, not *you*. Sure, it's risky to give up control, but so's not giving the child control. How will children learn the importance of their decisions if not on worthwhile, student-owned, age-appropriate, but not life-threatening, circumstances?

Your child heard the speaker. (Or maybe it's a teacher or counselor in a conference.) Save your thoughts. Don't rush in then or afterwards with your opinions and suggestions. Let your youngster talk about what he heard and thinks. React with non-committal nods and words. Listen and paraphrase. Recognize feelings as expressed.

As parents, we all seem to believe that by talking about the difficulty or importance of the *next* task or level of education, we're giving our students reasons to try harder. Only it doesn't work that way. What many children hear is: "What you've just done isn't good enough," or "I expect you to fail." People work harder and learn faster in an environment free from fear and anxiety.

Be encouraged. Your child's been learning and using school skills since she was born. Remember how she learned to sit up? Thousands of times she mentally and physically struggled to get upright before it became automatic.

Unfortunately, both you and your youngster may have been so anxious about her schoolwork that neither one of you has recognized other facets of her life where she is organized, persistent, and managing well.

Be encouraging. When the opportunity arises, remind her of a habit or skill she presently has that will be directly applicable to the more advanced assignments she'll be meeting. She spends hours on her bookcase while her room remains a disaster. Note her ability to organize and arrange material, to stay with a big undertaking.

She sticks a note on her mirror to remind herself of something. You say, "Hey, good thinking. You'll handle next year well."

She's anxious. You listen and later recall how last year she learned about breaking down her assignments into manageable portions (by using a desk calendar to schedule projects and time; organizing notebooks and material; or making use of the library and collecting information). "That's knowledge that counts," you tell her.

• Homework and Parental Assistance •

Effective parental assistance begins with the parent's consistent interest in a child's school life, availability for problem-solving sessions, and willingness to help with short-term homework.

Consistent interest does not mean asking your middle-school age child nightly about his assignments and making sure they're satisfactorily completed. It does mean listening and reflecting on anything your child has to say about his school life without moving into action.

Homework help often involves helping the child learn a difficult concept and checking his work after the knowledge has been applied to a particular assignment. It may include testing of memorized material, listening to a speech, proofreading a report, or assisting with the use of difficult reference material or equipment. If you work away from home, any assistance you give will necessarily occur during evening hours.

You and your child can consider this as you establish a distraction-free place reserved for doing homework and identify the best hours for its use. If your child decides not to do homework at the time you can help, remember your rights. Don't scold or blame. Be regretfully unavailable to help at other times or, if you so desire, suggest your child assist with, or do, one of your tasks so you can be available to help with the homework.

A discussion session can provide a setting in which to talk about homework. In discussion sessions, your aim is to treat your youngster as if she were already handling her school work responsibly.

This doesn't mean a hands-off, no participation position. It means giving your child a chance to think about the problem and consider with you, if she wishes, ideas and consequences. Then, since grades belong to her (and you believe her desire to do what is best for her own happiness is at least as strong as yours for her), she makes the choices and lives with the results.

Yes, she'll make some decisions that do not lead to her immediate happiness and well-being. All of us learn *not* to make bad decisions by experiencing the results that come from them.

Let's say a report card or progress report brings you word of a low or failing grade. Again, watch yourself for overreaction. Angry, judgmental words immediately indicate your emotional involvement in the outcome of the situation. They also place children on the defensive and encourage them to lie or argue for whatever position they decide is justified.

The grade directly affects your child. She is the only one with the power to make any solution to poor grades work. You want the natural consequences of this situation to belong to your child.

Youngsters do not want to fail. They may not do the work that would prevent it from happening, but every student with a failing grade believes until the last minute in miracles. Your youngster will tell you about this. Remain friendly, listening, and on your child's side.

Your reaction in a discussion about any school problem is important. When handled with your calm, nonjudgmental attention, it usually ends with an adolescent accepting, to a considerable degree, her responsibility for the situation.

• Effective Use of School Notices •

As soon as your child indicates her interest in problem solving, refer to the notice in your hand.

Notices. Printed or computer messages usually have letter grades or number percentages to indicate the level of a student's academic performance. These are followed by another series of words or phrases. From these the teacher checks the reasons that have led to her evaluation, both positively and negatively.

Check marks. Teachers put a great deal of time and thought into marking the word or phrase they feel most pinpoints a youngster's problem. Your youngster and the teacher were together in class—you were not there. Ask your child, "What do you think your teacher meant by checking 'effort'?" If he answers, "She means I should try harder," you could nod and wonder out loud how he would do that in science.

Choices. If he's thought about this and has ideas, write them down. Now you have something concrete and positive to discuss, ideas and plans from his mind that will help him reach his goal.

Discussions. Go slow; let him talk about his ideas, truthfully consider what behavior changes each will require of him, and the benefits each might bring.

Remember, your youngster is working to resolve an important problem in his life and he deserves your focused attention and time as he talks, but not your solutions. Use questions that require thoughtful answers. "How will that affect other parts of your life? How will you feel if that happens?"

Solutions. Adolescents, when given the opportunity, can come up with all kinds of possibilities. Your child may decide to give up a paper route or limit computer games, stay after school for teacher help, work with a tutor, or get more assistance from you. If the latter, be very clear about that which you will be doing under the guise of "assistance."

• Concentrate on Positive Behaviors •

If your youngster answers "I don't know" or "Nothing" when asked what he can do to improve his grade, look at other areas of his report card and focus on a subject he *is* handling satisfactorily. Even when counseling large numbers of children, only rarely did I find one performing poorly in *every* subject.

I recall saying to one student, "Joe, what did you do in your history class to get this B?" And he answered, "Laugh at the teacher's jokes and sit in the front seat." After we'd both grinned, he added, "Really, my papers aren't great, but I do get them in on time. I'm in my seat when the bell rings, and I like my teacher, so I listen when she explains stuff."

Now we had some basis for communicating. I could acknowledge he knew how to make good grades. I could show him the things I'd jotted down that he did in history and wonder how many of those things he didn't do in his science class.

"Well, I don't turn in all my assignments, but that's because I don't like science. Sometimes I get a paper half-finished and then forget about it."

Ah! Helpful information. Now we can talk about grade averaging. He can see me find the average of five grades of 60 and above, then do the same and change one 60 to a zero and let him see the striking difference it makes in his grade point average.

We can look at his list of "good" behaviors and wonder what underlying messages he conveys to his history teacher as he finishes his work, listens to her, and laughs at her jokes, and what messages he gives his science teacher when he doesn't. I can also note that while liking a subject or a teacher is nice, grades on daily work and tests are the only things that allow teachers to *put* grades on report cards.

• Hook into Your Child's Strengths •

As a school counselor, I could get Joe's cumulative-record folder and look at past report cards with him. I could note when he'd changed schools, been absent excessively, or had other problems. You can do the same with information you have about your child somewhere in a box or folder in your house. The middle school years are a good time for reviewing with your child his past school years.

As I opened Joe's folder, I asked him about the year he remembered as his best. He talked of his outstanding running ability in fourth grade, of a special teacher, and his parents still being together. Later, he noted his worst school year, of having to leave his regular classroom for periods of individual help, of changing schools in the middle of the year, and having a teacher he didn't like.

We talked about his standardized test scores and his percentile placement in the earlier grades compared to now; about his success in basketball; and what he said to himself about school, sports, friends, and teachers. We discussed the mental programming we do with ourselves for anything we tackle and how it affects our performance.

Can you see what we were doing?

We talked about years of Joe's life that affect him now, both positively and negatively. He read the comments his former teachers had written on his report cards and decided for himself whether they might be valid comments about him today. He had a chance to look at his past years, his strengths, and his weaknesses from his present, more mature position.

Finally, I noted again the responsibility he used in his history class, his self-discipline with his newspaper route, his willingness to practice for sports, and his honesty with me as we talked. "Now let's talk about a couple of things you might see yourself doing if you were to decide you wanted to make a better grade in that class."

Three weeks later the science teacher, who had originally referred Joe to me, stopped by my office to find out what kind of magic I'd sprinkled on this student.

It wasn't magic. I'd just invested an hour of my time and hooked Joe into his strengths that were there all the time.

Soon after my talk with Joe, one of the gifted young teachers at our school tossed an English homework paper on my desk and challenged me to read it. "Look at that new kid's handwriting. It's so terrible, I'm afraid to grade the test. Where do I begin?"

The new student's records had arrived and they showed that while her subject grades were average, every year her teachers commented about her poor writing. She'd been kept after school for special help, given follow-up drills for homework, and regularly received an unsatisfactory grade in penmanship. She had to know her penmanship was atrocious.

Full of the changes happening at our house as we were trying to limit our criticism and notice the positive, I wondered if the teacher, Mr. G., would like to try a similar approach with this youngster. "We know children who have been functioning poorly in an area over an extended period of time become deeply discouraged, often believing they are incapable of changing. Maybe you could begin with anything you see that's positive rather than all that you and she both know is negative."

We talked about the fact that children, particularly those unaccustomed to success, often respond poorly to enthusiastic doses of praise. I shared with him my findings on chores and the obvious advantage I'd found in using an honest, low-key, specific "I" reaction message to a positive, observable behavior.

Recognizing the possibility that her other teachers might be equally as concerned about her handwriting, a memo was sent to each explaining Mr. G.'s attention to the problem and asking that they resist commenting unless they noticed an improvement and wanted to react specifically to that. I also recommended that all communication about her writing be done in a private setting or inconspicuously on her papers.

Some weeks later this caring teacher stopped to show me the student's latest paper. I was amazed at her handwriting. "How did you do it?" I gasped.

"I didn't. She did it." He shook his head in wonderment. "The day you and I talked, I met with her after school, and showed her some words I'd underlined on her papers. I told her they were all ones I found easy to read and wondered if she could tell me why.

"By the time she'd finished, she'd given me five good reasons. I chuckled and told her it seemed she knew how to write, all she had to do was move her knowledge to more words." He'd suggested she choose one of the five handwriting skills he'd listed as she talked and be conscious of using that one skill in as many words as possible for a while.

"Your handwriting grade will be on just that one skill. As soon as it becomes a habit in your fingers, as well as knowledge in your head, you'll know. Then you can choose another skill to think about."

The teacher could scarcely contain his delight. "By the second week she was joining the letters in every word, spacing them correctly, and keeping them on the line so well her other teachers were beginning to notice. Now she's used up the original five skills and is working on more sophisticated ones. You see the results and I don't even understand it!"

I'm not saying we can all move instantly into these positive thinking comments and meaningful discussions with our youngsters. It takes practice to learn to communicate on this level. However, beginning this kind of talk with school behavior allows your child to think about past frustrations, behavior, grades, values, peer pressure, and responsibility. All are things that affect his life.

The reason good school counseling works so well is that student and counselor have a topic of common interest. You too only need the time to talk and a topic your child cares about—one you can discuss without judgment, anger, or control.

School Problems

• Steps to Change •

Recognize inappropriate emotions. Physically separate yourself from your child. Take time to consider the old situations, emotions, and beliefs that may have affected your response.

Use your new understanding. Share your insights about your feelings with your child. Listen to his explanations with an open mind. Do not judge his future success by the mistakes he makes as an adolescent.

Be involved but not in control. Avoid instant advice, negative comments, and lectures. Encourage homework independence. Treat your child as you would if she were already a responsible student.

Hook your adolescent into her strengths. Recognize past accomplishments. Note your child's use of positive, transferable skills, such as the ability to plan, persist, be on time, organize, and listen.

Keep choices and consequences in your child's hands. Let your child experience the results of his decisions without parental interference.

9

Resistance and Acceptance

New Belief: *The ideas and limitations we verbalize as facts quickly become the beliefs that shape our abilities, feelings, and behavior.*

• Identifying Problem Behavior •

One weekend I attended a workshop for counselors. We were to learn, by participation, about changing problem behavior.

After a few minutes of get-acquainted and relaxation exercises, the leader asked us to close our eyes and think of a negative behavior we had each tried unsuccessfully to change in ourselves. "Now," he said, "recall how you routinely behave when you are acting out this behavior."

My choice was easy. I'd just gained several pounds and I knew why. I could see myself taking three pieces of the fudge a daughter had recently made, and then, before the hour was out, three more! "I can't resist it," I'd explain apologetically.

The next day in the theater I bought chocolate bars, muttering as I did, "I can't help it. They make the movie for me." At school, I lamented my fondness for the chocolate cake served in the cafeteria and then chose the largest piece. Our children teased me about pilfering their Halloween treats and my inability to resist anyone's chocolate-chip cookies.

The leader interrupted my thoughts, "Now think of the words you were just using to justify your habit and convince yourself you couldn't change." I was astonished. Every utterance I made about chocolate reinforced my helplessness in the face of this weakness.

The leader then pointed out to us that the area in our brain that collects and stores information does not have the ability to distinguish between fact or fiction, truth or lies. Instead, it takes the information we repeatedly put forth, neatly saves it with other information on the subject, and returns it to us for our use the next time we face a similar situation. We then shared in small groups our earliest memories of our problem behavior and its later growth.

Monday morning, I literally gasped when I saw the huge box of candy sitting on the receptionist's desk in the counseling area. At the same moment, a co-worker dashed over, lifted its cover and said, "A parent brought this after you left Friday. You're going to love them. They're all chocolate!"

The leader's words rang in my ears, "Truth or lie, fact or fiction, it makes no difference. It is all stored!" I decided to react differently and give my brain new information.

"Oh," I mumbled, trying not to look in the box. "Something chocolate made me sick last week. Maybe later," I said, moving quickly into my office. Breathing deeply, I closed the door and leaned against it.

I'd taken the first step, but could I really change my chocolate craving just by giving my mind new information to store? Five pounds of candy would last all week, even with everyone eating it. Everyday I'd be going in and out, seeing it, smelling it, hearing others enjoy it! How could I possibly resist it?

• Reprogramming Our Brains •

All right, counselor, work on yourself. I knew that the weight lifter under hypnosis who suddenly acquired the ability to lift 25 extra pounds didn't do it through new muscles. He'd simply acquired through the hypnotist a new belief about his *ability* to lift.

What would give my brain an equally strong message about the undesirability of those chocolates? Suddenly, from my growing-up years in Florida, the picture of a large flying cockroach flashed into my mind.

Imagination is a powerful tool when we put our visualization skills into action. Now the repulsive thought of a boxful of chocolate-covered, dead cockroaches was so vivid it totally, if momentarily, replaced the picture I'd previously held of the cream-and-nut mixtures actually there.

What a powerful attention getter! Could such a potent visualization help me erase the old information I'd sent for years to the storage facility in my brain? The idea was fascinating.

Each day, I found new ways of avoiding the always offered, ever-present candy. Every time I refused, the next refusal was easier. "I'm too full. I've just finished a big lunch, . . . just brushed my teeth. Not today, guess my taster's changed. Hmmm, no, chocolate doesn't appeal to me anymore."

Lies? Yes, but I said them repeatedly as if they were true, and they helped. So did the undesirable mental pictures I continued to create about what was just beneath the chocolate coating. I was constantly giving myself new facts about chocolate's undesirability and my relationship to it.

One day walking through a mall, I found myself automatically refusing some free samples of chocolate candy. It wasn't a question of liking it or not, I just didn't want it. It was nothing more than any ordinary food. I could take it or leave it.

• The Complaining Habit •

What would happen if I listened sensitively to our children's emotional and controversial statements, just as the group leader listened to me when I talked of my early feelings about chocolate? I'd been trying to do this on the big things the children were bringing home, those I was able to designate as belonging to them, but how about their daily complaints and argumentative resistance?

It wasn't simple. She said, "I hate these exercises. I don't need them!" And I answered, "Yes, you do, you heard the doctor!" He declared, "No breakfast for me, I'm getting fat." And before I could stop myself I said, "It's already cooked, eat! You're not fat, just look at your feet, you're going to be tall!"

They said, "I hate church, yard work, going to Grandma's, practicing." They insisted, "Everyone cuts, buys that brand, drinks, goes to concerts, and rides their bikes there." It was one issue after another, yet all my efforts to convince them otherwise only elicited more evidence to support their positions. "It's dumb, boring, too hard. You don't understand." No matter how minor the subject, it seemed they had to argue about it with us.

Many of the situations involved problems where ownership areas weren't clear. We owned some parts because of their age, our finances, or the consequences we'd experience. Other parts, while rightly belonging to them, we still couldn't release.

Clearly, however, my statements justifying my love of chocolate and my increasing belief over the years that I could not resist it, had kept me a prisoner of chocolate. As I attempted to refute the children's complaints, did I, at the same time, place them in a position of having to argue for the very stance I wanted them to give up?

It was an interesting thought and almost immediately life's circumstances brought me more supporting evidence for the idea.

• Total Resistance •

During Clif's serious illness and his time at home, he willingly helped with family management by doing many of the things I'd previously handled. However, he would never prepare a real meal. His practice at dinner time was to rotate us night after night through hot dogs, hamburgers, TV dinners, frozen pot pies, canned chili, and jars of spaghetti sauce.

With the older two now in college, the middle ones busy with after-school jobs, and the younger two really too young to handle meals, we all felt his assistance in real meal planning and cooking was mandatory. Unfortunately, all our problem-solving, one-on-one private talks, and carefully thought out "I" messages were heard, acknowledged, and *not* acted upon.

In desperation, one Friday evening Barbara and Teresa openly confronted him about his unwillingness to prepare wholesome, varied meals. He avoided the real issue and simply indicated that, while he knew we weren't happy with his way of feeding us, it was the best he could do. If we didn't like it, we'd have to work out some change among ourselves.

On hearing these words, Barbara, our outspoken, liberated teenager, let loose with all the pent-up frustration she'd been harboring for weeks, ending with, "If this is marriage, and this is what you call love, then I want no part of it. I'm never getting married!"

• Total Acceptance •

Suddenly, logic didn't matter. Barbara wasn't talking about Clif's cooking, she was criticizing our marriage and our life. "Wait!" I said. "Whether your father cooks meals or not says absolutely nothing to me about his love. In fact, maybe he *can't* cook because all these years of *my* cooking has said so much to him about my love!"

My voice was so resolute no one even moved. "Whatever his reason, his cooking is a topic no longer up for discussion in our house. Your dad does a hundred other things that are more important to my happiness and our marriage than cooking. He doesn't cook, so be it. Subject closed forever!"

My perspective was totally clear and everyone knew it. Meals would be prepared by other people, and that was all right. Grinning at my own fierceness, I hooked my hand through Clif's arm and said, "How about hot dogs cooked in the fireplace?"

What happened as a result of my outburst? Monday night we came home to the wonderful smell of pot roast, potatoes, and carrots cooking in the oven, and Clif, full of smiles and amazement, saying as I walked in, "I don't know why, but today I felt different. I could cook. I even *wanted* to cook!"

In counseling work, I knew the power for change a client could receive over time from the acceptance of his behavior by a caring therapist. Did my outburst have this effect on Clif?

Could an unexpected and genuine acceptance of our position by someone who means a great deal to us somehow break the emotional chains that have bound us to our position?

Had my positive and dramatic words of truth flushed from Clif's brain old, stored beliefs—just as my visualization and the positive, but untrue, statements I made about chocolate had changed my longstanding belief that I couldn't resist it? So it seemed.

• New Insights, New Words •

I had to try my new learning with our children in their everyday lives, so full of complaints and opposition. I began by talking less and responding with a monosyllabic or neutral response to their controversial, negative words, saying, "Oh?" "My!" "Ah." Or I used just sounds of acknowledgment: "Yes," "Hmmm,"

"Huh." Or a low-key sentence that indicated I was hearing but not judging: "I guess we do seem uptight about money." "It could seem everyone but you gets to ride a bike there." "It could appear, sound, look . . ."

Soon I was starting many of my responses to controversial statements with a "Yes" and then giving the follow-up restatement of their problem or situation: "Yes, it is rough being the oldest." "Yes, it's hard doing exercises and not seeing any results." "Yes, it is, it does, it could, it must, it might . . ." This process was rather like getting one's feet in the right position for a good golf swing. The follow-through paraphrasing of the emotions and descriptions of problems in our houseful of varied temperaments began to flow naturally.

———

My daughter slammed the door and threw her books on the floor. "We must be the poorest people in town. Our station wagon's a mess. It's horrible!"

"Yes, it is pretty old," I murmured, moving near her.

Her voice dropped. "I could have died today when Dad picked me up from play practice! The car rattled as he came down the block, and inside the car, . . . Mommm!"

"Yes, kids, stuff, papers, crumbs . . ."

"And Dad brings them with him every time. They're always there, hanging out the windows, giggling, listening, fighting!"

I pushed her hair from her face and nodded. "Living in a big family isn't easy, is it?"

———

Just listening took care of some of the children's anger. They needed to complain and express their frustrations, but I didn't have to right the apparent wrong or change the situation.

Our son might have quit church the year he began to complain about attending, but I didn't argue with him once. Instead, as I listened in a "Yes" frame of mind while he described the "science fiction" aspects of our Christian faith, the "repetitious dogma" in some of the minister's sermons, and the unnecessary formality we placed on him with Sunday clothes and behavior, I began to appreciate the serious thought he was giving to religion and his own beliefs. A year later when he did insist on not attending church, I was ready. His action didn't mean his spiritual growth was ending. My new practice of acceptance and agreement was working well for my peace of mind.

• Listening Brings Understanding •

Obviously, though, there was more for me to learn. In the middle of what I thought was a stimulating Saturday morning discussion with Clif, he suddenly stood up and asked me why I had to argue with him on every single issue. "It doesn't matter what I say, you disagree!"

"Me? Arguing all the time? Why, I'm the least argumentative person in this family!" I declared.

"Then listen to yourself, what are you doing right now?" he asked, as he stalked out of the room.

In no way could I buy his accusation. I was just trying to keep a conversation going. I'd show him. I'd just let him do all the talking for a while and see how he liked that!

After the seven o'clock news, Clif shook his head and remarked, "It sure looks like the president wants us in a war."

Instantly, the words were in my mouth, "How can you say that? No president wants war." Then I swallowed them. No! Gently now, watch your tone. "What a scary thought. I hope not. What makes you think this?" I asked.

"Look," he said, reaching for the current issues of two news magazines and opening them to pages where he'd underlined some paragraphs. For several minutes, he summarized for me the foreign policy steps the president had taken during the last months and other comments he'd read in editorials and heard on news shows. Now the president's quick, almost inconspicuous action today took on new importance to me.

Did my instant, opinionated responses often place me so immediately in a position contrary to Clif's that I didn't give him a chance to say what he had to say, or hear, open-mindedly, what he did say?

All week, I watched myself and avoided refuting his statements or even presenting my ideas and opinions the first time he brought up a subject. Our every conversation made my heart hurt. How little I'd been listening to the ideas he casually brought forth.

Our talks at mealtime, our trips to the doctor, and our around-the-house chatter began to be different.

He wondered casually what I thought of some structural changes he was thinking of making in the garage. Instantly, my mind flew to the mess and trouble involved, then I caught myself. That could come tomorrow, even an hour from now, if he wanted to act fast. "Yes, we should be thinking of earthquake safety. Tell me about your ideas."

After looking at his sketches and cost estimates, I murmured, "It's all so detailed, I'll bet you've been thinking about this for days." He laughed, "Would you believe months?"

A week later as I left for work, Clif followed me to the car, turned me toward him, and said, "Just in case you're interested, I've noticed. It's like the difference between night and day!" Could it be that if I didn't have to be right, I didn't have to argue?

———

Della, our oldest daughter, came home for Christmas, and as usual, arrived from college full of controversial comments about everything from our government's handling of war to the advantages of cohabitation before marriage. With good intentions, we tried to stay calm and refute her radical statements with facts and reasoning.

Unfortunately, these were highly emotional topics and every communication seemed to escalate into an argument. Worst of all, these were not intellectual discussions. Each was so firmly committed to a particular position that no one wanted to hear what anyone else had to say. Any statement from one threw the other automatically into an angry position of defense or attack.

After she left, Clif and I resolved to change our reaction to the combative statements this daughter continually threw at us. We would not take a position about anything the first time she brought up a topic for discussion. Later, we would state our view, that which *we were sure* was the truth. Maybe by then she'd be able to consider it.

Her next visit was Valentine's Day weekend. Two hours after her arrival a large box of candy given to the family disappeared. When someone asked about it, she answered, "It's too much sugar! I've put it away and I'll bring it out again as soon as everyone reads this paper on the dangers of sugar."

Instantly, I was ready for battle. How dare she force her opinions on us like this? Then Clif caught my eye, and his expression reminded me of our agreement: *Don't take a position on anything the first time it comes up for discussion.*

I clenched my teeth. Then with Clif grinning at my control, I repositioned my mouth into a smile, and quite cheerfully said, "All right, we'll read it and maybe we'll learn something." It seems such a minor statement now, but it wasn't then.

We'd given all our children desserts everyday of their lives, how could sugar be bad? What about all those lunch-box cookies, Popsicles and lollipops, those birthday celebrations, and holiday treats? How could we consider them unhealthy, even deadly? What would that say about us?

We read Della's paper and listened to her back-up arguments. We paraphrased her thoughts and conceded researchers *were* finding out new things everyday about nutrition, blood sugar, and health. We listened as she talked about red meat and additives, army generals who distort figures and facts, oil companies who exploit, about contaminated water, and the possibility that our country's position could be wrong on one thing or another.

We didn't attempt to refute anything she said all weekend, and a strange feeling of benevolence developed among the three of us. It was as if she were a friend, one we cared for deeply but whose opinions, beliefs, and values were hers to speak and own. We really had no responsibility for changing them. We just listened.

The day she left, we found a note on the table telling us we'd find in the garage a box of canned goods and packaged items she'd removed from our kitchen shelves. "Please, just read their labels and notice the placement of sugar in the list of ingredients. I'm not trying to make you stop using sugar. I just want you to know how much is unnecessarily being put into supposedly healthy food."

The next week, there was a loving follow-up letter suggesting we read the book she was sending us about the large amounts of sugar the average American was now consuming compared to earlier years. It related sugar to certain diseases on the increase and the definite changes it created in body chemistry.

By the time we finished the book, our idea of truth had changed, not hers. Was this new evidence of how opinionated and judgmental words lock us into a position from which change is difficult or impossible?

106

Resistance and Acceptance

• Steps to Change •

Recognize the power of words and beliefs. Our brains store what they hear without pausing to determine truth or validity. A person arguing for his beliefs or limitations soon comes to believe them.

Decide to reduce family conflict and resistence. Avoid opposing a subject the first time it is presented. Listen for points of agreement. If you don't have to be right, there won't be an argument.

Be alert to negative responses. Words that blame, judge, or control encourage defensiveness and exaggerated statements about needs, feelings, and limitations.

Take a positive stance. Note your child's knowledge, thinking, and concern about the subject. Develop an interest in differing opinions. Save your other viewpoints until a later time.

Experiment with total acceptance. Emotionally and intellectually accept the situation totally as the other person sees it. Verbalize your honest acceptance. Take an action that indicates clearly your acceptance.

10

Understanding Teen Sexuality

New Belief: *We must become as committed to discussing sexual matters and the multitude of experiences in life that influence our children's sexual behavior as we are in discussing other home, school, health, and safety issues.*

• Present-Day Sexual Behavior •

Half of all graduating high-school students report that they have already been sexually active. That fact, plus the large number of pregnancies and sexually transmitted diseases occurring among our teenagers, requires us to face the truth. Our children are growing up in a cultural climate where a large portion of the general population accepts sexual intercourse as a natural and healthy part of unmarried, as well as married couples' relationships.

When I asked a 17-year-old what boys were saying to girls now to get them to have sex, she took so long to think about it I finally suggested, "If you really loved me, you would?" She looked up, amazed at my words. "They'd never say that. You see, it's not true. They know girls have sex just because they want to have sex."

The cultural sanction to have sex has always existed for adolescent males; now it is just as much an option for females. Whether you or I agree with this view or not, our children accept it. If they personally do not believe they should have sex, they still believe it's all right for their peers. This means their decisions regarding their own behavior are situationally based and open to change.

For at least half of our children the question seems to be not if, but how soon.

Understanding and responding to our children's growing sexuality is tremendously difficult for most parents. I was no exception. On a quiet, teenless Sunday night while looking for the latest issue of a magazine, I remembered that an adolescent daughter had been reading it earlier. Not finding it lying around, I opened the top drawer of her bedside stand. There it was.

I picked it up and before me lay a medically prescribed contraceptive for women and a supply of drugstore condoms. I was stunned!

What was our teenage daughter doing with all this birth control stuff? She was too young for sex! What did she know about having that kind of a relationship with anyone! To my knowledge, she wasn't even that involved with the boy she was currently "seeing."

Suddenly, I was furious. In almost one movement, I yanked the drawer from the stand, dumped its contents onto her bed, and scribbled on a large piece of paper, "I hate this! Hate it, hate it, hate it! What are you planning to do, try out every boy in your crowd?"

This is not the way I wish I'd reacted, but if I want you to realize how difficult it is for parents to use good skills in the challenges their children bring to them as they grow, I have to be honest.

I was in bed when she came home, but for both of us it was a night of smoldering anger that erupted into hurtful words the next morning. She felt I'd deliberately invaded her privacy and was outraged at my action. My efforts to defend my behavior escalated into further attacks on hers. I left almost immediately for work.

Fortunately a school nurse, who was a friend and parent of daughters herself, joined me in my office and "listened with her heart" as I poured out my story. It took a while. We're so vulnerable when it comes to matters of our children's sexuality.

• Talking Doesn't Come Naturally •

We're the parents, experienced and knowledgeable (to varying degrees) in these areas, but we still have difficulty discussing in depth with our teenager those intimate, sexual feelings and behaviors many of us believe should be reserved for adulthood.

We resist the idea that our young teenager and his/her equally young friend will experience those all-consuming, passionate feelings that make kissing, necking, and petting stepping stones to intercourse. It's even more unacceptable to think such behavior could begin with nothing more than curiosity or the desire to experience for themselves a forbidden, yet highly promoted, adult behavior.

As parents we know well the "live-now, grow-up-fast" messages our children receive from the media; from world-renowned, teen-idolized adult figures; and from their sexually active peers. We realize that to an adolescent, having sex may seem the single most direct action she can take to move into instant adulthood. But we're caught in a bind. If we talk as if it can happen, aren't we somehow encouraging it to happen?

Many parents believe that their moral values, religious teachings, and home rules will prevent their children from becoming sexually active. These parents do not engage in explicit sex-education discussions with their early teenage children or talk with them about the possibility of their ever having sex as adolescents.

Other parents feel secure because they have studiously prepared their child for the physical and emotional changes that come with puberty and have told them of the difficulties and responsibilities early sexual experience brings. They may even have said those truthful, frightening words: "There is no absolutely safe way of having sex. When intercourse occurs, pregnancy or a sexually transmitted disease is always a possibility."

We all want to believe that whatever we are doing will keep our adolescent children committed to abstinence until they finish high school, go to college, live on their own, or get married. We want to keep the reality of today's sexual attitudes out of our homes, but we can't.

As my friend and I talked, I realized how my words had reflected my desires for our daughter. I had judged her behavior from the point of view of my beliefs, values, and the culture I had experienced in my growing up. She was taking a different path. I had to touch her heart before I could hope to again communicate with her mind.

A change of attitude often benefits from a deed involving action as well as talk. In a letter, I explained my insights, apologized for my angry, hurting words, and recognized the mature responsibility my daughter was taking by her wise and healthy planning for sex. I recalled other times in her life when she'd made good decisions in difficult situations and expressed my appreciation of the thought she'd given to this one. I delivered it to her during her afternoon job.

That night, our daughter let me see the needless damage of my judgmental words. She wasn't, as yet, sexually involved with anyone, but neither was she going to wait for marriage. She didn't know whether she was in love or not, or even if she'd wait until she was in love to have sex. She liked this boy a lot and she wasn't going to be caught unprepared. A friend had been unprepared and an abortion had been her answer to an unwanted pregnancy. Later, when I asked our daughter why she'd not given me any indication she was considering such a big step in her life, her answer was quick, "Because you'd have flipped out, just like you did. Mom, this isn't something you'd have wanted to talk to me about doing—only, not doing!"

• Communicate! •

Our aim must be to discuss and consider all issues involving sexual behavior so rationally and openly with our adolescent children that they'll know we're capable of handling their sexual confidences and concerns of a personal nature equally as well.

Adolescents do not complain about receiving too much sexual information from their parents, only too little. They know that they have not reached full maturity despite their early sexual development, apparent sophistication of knowledge, and breadth of choices. They still need and want caring parent participation in their ongoing sexual growth, but they need it before we think they're ready to need it.

Our children's sexuality is a complex mixture of physical, emotional, and social factors. Sexual maturity develops over years of time that are not equivalent with any two children. Initiating conversations on "adult" sexual issues should begin during our children's preteen years.

When good growth and development or "sex ed" classes are part of the elementary and middle-school curriculum, they can have a tremendous impact on children. Parents, however, cannot count on classes to answer all their child's needs for information. The material taught, movies shown, and discussions held may be meaningful and well presented, yet still have little lasting impact on a particular individual. Children bring to these classes their own background of knowledge, fears, and sexual experiences. For everyone it's sensitive material, difficult to understand, and not easy to remember.

Parents can reinforce the school's efforts by being informed about the material covered, and then bringing up, occasionally, a *specific topic* for family discussion. Bringing up information children may have heard before in light of new information is easy. "I know they talked about sexually transmitted diseases in your sex ed class, but an article I was reading recently mentioned venereal warts as a problem. What have you heard about them?"

It's part of a parent's job to encourage their children to make healthy, growth-producing choices that will benefit them and the society in which they live. If you believe in delaying sexual activity, then talk about the kind of values you hope your adolescent will honor and do it long before she is faced with making a decision that will affect those standards. Discuss the positive health, growth, social, and religious reasons for your beliefs, and support them with current research and informative articles.

The more an adolescent understands about her choices and the consequences of each, the better her chance of making a healthy, growth-producing choice.

Adolescents are intensely caught up emotionally in the things that are happening to them in their everyday lives. Consider with them some of the situations that bring pressure on a teen's commitment to high standards. These might include social activities involving the use of alcohol or drugs, parties where adults are not present, and dates where there's too much privacy. It's also important to talk about those adolescent gatherings with their shared confidences where early sexual activity is discussed and encouraged.

You can't prevent such activities from occurring, but you can alert your youngster to situations that weaken resolve. The situations above bring excitement, group acceptance, and the closeness of friendship into a young person's life. They influence adolescent choices.

Discussions that deal with options and choices rather than "do or don't" behavior are easier for adolescents to handle. Ask your daughter if she can recall a time when a friend tried to talk her into doing something she didn't want to do and despite the friend's repeated requests, she never agreed to do it. If she shares with you how she managed the incident, acknowledge the effectiveness of her method and the strong information she has now stored in her brain about what works for her.

One youngster, continually urged by her best friend to cut school during lunch hour, handled it all year with some version of, "Not today, today's just not a good day for me." Finally one day the friend said, "Is any day ever going to be a good day for you to cut?" And of course, her answer was, "No, I really don't want to miss my classes."

Strength comes through small steps, repeatedly taken.

• Topics for Sexual Discussions •

While adolescents do not take sex casually, they rarely come to parents asking directly for information. Decide now to make any sexual issue acceptable for family talk.

We dramatically increase our opportunities to communicate with a teen when we keep our attention generally focused on her/ his position, feelings, and beliefs rather than on our own.

Effective conversation with teens involves bringing up topics from the daily, grown-up, sexual environment in which they live, and then listening as they express their thoughts and beliefs on the varying subjects. It means being willing to talk about sexual curiosity and desire; about safety from sexual assault, sexually transmitted diseases, and pregnancy. It involves talking about sexual roles and sexual activity at school, work, and home; about sexual activity when it is connected to alcohol and drugs; about "being in love" and the responsibilities and consequences of such an intimate relationship.

All you need is a starting item. Look in magazines or newspapers for articles involving date-rape, statistics on preteen and adolescent sexuality, homosexuality, sexual harassment or abuse, dating skills, and finally the specific sexual behavior happening in and around your local schools and communities.

Develop an interest in your children's everyday activities. Listen to the songs they hear, jot down some of the lyrics and choose a time for talking about what they mean. Watch movies and television programs with your teens. At first, it may seem embarrassing or unfitting to discuss directly the sexual scene you and your son witnessed on a television or movie screen. Recognize, however, that you saw it together and both of you were affected by it in some way. You'll both gain from talking about it.

Avoid giving your immediate opinion about the topics you bring up for discussions. Instead, say easily, "I keep thinking about that article in the paper today on the date-rape that happened at J. B. High School. Have you and your friends talked about how it could happen?" Or, "When is it, or is it not, rape?" Try to be comfortable with any opinions your child offers and resist debating their value. Take all feelings and comments seriously. Do a lot of paraphrasing and listening.

When we judge negatively a teenager's choices and opinions, we're criticizing her judgment and that leads to arguments rather than discussions.

Even though our *older* adolescent children want parent participation in their lives, they quickly become resistant to discussions that end up with the parent telling them what's right or wrong. If you believe in certain values, have lived them, and have talked with your children about your reasons for holding them as true, then your children know how you feel and what you want. They're now concerned about their beliefs, feelings, and the choices they know they will eventually make for themselves.

There is no research that supports the idea that talking about any sexual matter, including the use of contraceptives, with a responsible adult encourages an adolescent to become sexually active. Instead, it's far more likely, as with other situations involving difficult decisions, that the more information a teenager has about sexual matters, the better these situations will be handled.

Our aim is to view all sexual topics as worthwhile, interesting subjects for comfortable conversation. If such talk can become natural to us and routine in our homes, perhaps we'll not leave our children's education in the hands of others by default.

• Sexual Attack from an Unknown Person •

Sexual safety: We want it so badly for our children and yet every newspaper and nightly broadcast tells us there's no way we can ensure it. Even those children who live in what we consider safe neighborhoods and are well versed in safety behavior can be taken suddenly by force or enticed into a dangerous situation by an ingenious attacker.

———

Our pretty, seventh-grade daughter stepped out of the school bus and began a three-block walk down a local street that led into our area. It had a few homes on one side and an overgrown hillside and horse paddock on the other. She left the bus with other students, but they went in different directions.

A man with a tripod and camera stepped out of a car parked on the hill side of the street and called to her. "I'm a magazine photographer and I'm taking pictures in this area. How about posing for a few?"

It sounded plausible, harmless, and fun to her. After taking several shots, he suggested she put her schoolbooks down for the next photo. Talking all the time about his work, he straightened her collar and shifted her position to a different spot. This happened several times before she suddenly realized they'd moved to a higher level where bushes and trees blocked them from anyone's street or stable view.

She turned abruptly, hurried downhill, picked up her books, and said she really had to go. "Sure," he said, "but how about one more shot? Then you can give me your name and address and I'll send you prints of the pictures."

She agreed and he again set up his tripod and adjusted her position and clothes. Suddenly, the hand on her waist tightened and the other moved beneath her skirt and into her underwear. Terrified, our daughter screamed, "Don't you touch me," as she twisted from his grasp, hit him with her books, and ran.

Busy lives or troubled home situations may encourage silence rather than sharing of frightening experiences. That day our family was getting an older teen packed and transported to an out-of-town college. We didn't hear about our seventh grader's danger until 24 hours later! It's difficult for our adolescents themselves to accept their growing sexuality and vulnerability. Even though our daughter knew we would not blame her for the experience, she blamed herself. She'd talked to a stranger and then let him talk her into an unsafe situation with his impressive job and flattering words. Didn't that somehow make her responsible for the danger, too?

Later, her descriptions to the police were accurate and helpful and she was able to identify her attacker, a well-respected businessman, in a police picture line-up. Our daughter escaped injury, but the room at the grand jury hearing was filled with other similarly attractive young girls who had been molested or raped by a nice looking "photographer" who used hillside settings for his violence.

———

We must never think attacks by strangers are rare events. They're not. They happen in every community and in some areas they happen everyday. Talking about avoiding the aggression that comes from strangers is tremendously important, but so is the safety behavior we model. We lock our doors and do not open them to strangers. We do not leave our young children unsupervised in public and private situations. We consider with our child the safety of a walking area before we approach it. We never pick up hitchhikers. If your teen comments about the hitchhiker's innocent appearance, tell her that when the pictures of hitchhikers who rob, attack, and murder were mixed with pictures of law-abiding people, the pictures of the criminals were chosen as threatening no more often than those of the others.

We make talking about the safety of life a day-to-day business with our children. We talk about problems that can happen as they walk to school, cross a parking lot, enter or leave a place of employment. We encourage the buddy system for bike rides, walks, and even trips to a public bathroom. We talk about the reports of aggression in our local papers and wonder how attacks could have been avoided. We think and talk about safety and we plan for it.

Despite all this care, the worst can happen. "Just this once," perhaps, a youngster picks up a hitchhiker or hitchhikes herself, takes the shortcut through the park at dusk, or goes out with someone she's just met at the bowling alley. Even though anger at her thoughtless behavior may almost immediately take over your emotions, let that anger and pain be focused directly on the aggressor's behavior. When it comes to matters of safety all of us use poor judgment at times. That doesn't mean we're to blame for someone else's illegal and immoral acts of violence.

If your child has suffered a devastating experience, she is already full of self-blame and guilt. Hold and love her without judgmental questions and statements that benefit from your hindsight. Be grateful she is alive, that she kept her head about her to whatever level she did. Encourage her to talk about the situation, and stay with her and listen with all the skills you've been learning.

No matter how difficult the experience is for you, it is unbelievably worse for your child. Keep the lines of communication open between you. You are her first source of strength. The more she can talk about her experience, the better she will be. She needs to relive how it happened again and again. Give her time to grieve over her losses—both physical and emotional—that she has experienced and grieve with her yourself. At the very least, your daughter's trust in others and her confidence in her own ability to protect herself have been shattered.

There is no quick healing of damage that sexual aggression creates. Your child, you, and possibly other family members will benefit greatly from getting professional counseling as soon as possible.

• Sexual Abuse from a Known Person •

A sexual attack by a stranger is always devastating and life-threatening, but sexual abuse by a trusted person adds a new dimension of tragedy to the victim's experience.

As a school counselor, many of the sexual abuse situations that have come to my attention have been ongoing. The children were long-time victims, trapped in another person's behavior, and afraid to report it. They were usually referred to me by a caring, observant teacher who recognized that something was very wrong in the child's life.

Such children are battered emotionally and physically and are often threatened with serious consequences to themselves or others in their family if they talk about their problems to anyone. Victims of such abuse are also afraid the adult they most likely would tell won't believe what they say, or will blame them for some part of it.

It's terrible for us to think that someone we know, and possibly love, would sexually molest or assault our child, but it happens everyday to some child. We need to face the truth that sexual abuse happens to children in families from good homes, with caring parents, relatives, neighbors, friends, and community workers.

Known child molesters look and act just like we do—most of the time.

Children almost never lie to a parent about sexual abuse. Always assume that your child is telling you the truth and express instantly your total love and support for him. Let him know that your anger and indignation are all directed towards the molester. Do not ask your child questions that place blame, such as, "Why didn't you leave the first time he touched you?" or, "Why didn't you tell me right away?"

You saw the difficulty our daughter had in handling the approach of an unknown, but responsible appearing, adult. Imagine how much harder it is to recognize and resist a beloved family member, coach, clergyman, or baby-sitter who talks about the activity being all right or just an enjoyable game they're playing.

After hearing about such a situation and reacting with love, support, and belief, then focus your attention on what the child did right, rather than what she did wrong. Tell her, "You did the right thing. You told someone about what happened. Even though you were hurt and frightened, you told someone."

After a 3-year-old was fondled sexually by the husband of a home nursery-school owner, the little girl waited until she was out of the house and then looking directly into her father's eyes, she said, "I don't like the daddy who lives there. Don't take me there again!"

Obviously, these parents had previously given their child the message that her feelings about adults were important and would be honored. If we want our children to develop their own inner sensitivity to unacceptable adult behavior, we need to listen to their early, hard-to-explain fears and feelings and respond to them as supportively as these parents did their daughter's.

We can't prevent many of the things that happen to our children. We must, however, talk to our children about self-protection in all kinds of situations and let them know we want them to be sensitive to any sexual behavior from another person that makes them feel uncomfortable.

It is particularly important that our preadolescent and early teenage children understand that this includes unwanted sexual behavior of any kind from boyfriends, acquaintances, and the friends of siblings and parents. Contrary to what the 17-year-old at the beginning of this chapter felt was her freedom of choice in sexual matters, many of our younger girls experience intense peer pressure, and even coercion, for sexual activity from males their own age and older.

Middle-school age boys do ask 11- and 12-year-old girls if they're still virgins and then mock them for holding to their "grandma" beliefs. A boy may talk to a girl attending her first school dance about "real kisses," touch her breasts, and talk graphically about what he'd like to do with her later. If the girl doesn't respond, he may question her femininity and then tease, or directly threaten, to tell his friends she "did," even though she "didn't."

Girls bring pressure on their female friends and on reluctant boys, as well. Those who have become sexually active talk about it positively and encourage others in the same behavior. The more group members who participate in an adult-opposed behavior the more acceptable it becomes to everyone in the group.

Youngsters, particularly girls, have unwanted sex and do not think of calling it rape. Sex may happen through manipulation or fear, alcohol or drug use, or force, but it happens even when the girl or boy says no. The aggressors do not call it rape either. They say, "She led me on and then resisted," or "She did it with her old boyfriend, what did she expect?" or "She said 'no' but she really meant 'yes,'" or "He's a boy, so of course he wanted to have sex." We need to talk to our boys *and* our girls about the unfair, immoral, and illegal aspects of having sex with anyone who does not want it or is under the age of legal consent.

We want to talk to our adolescents about a slower path to intimacy—one that allows our adolescents to grow through wholesome activities, good conversation, and a world of exciting life challenges that do not require sexual activity, drugs, or alcohol for their success.

Finally, let's not just talk about healthy emotional growth. Let's show our adolescents through our lives the loving effort, trust, shared communication, respect, and emotional closeness that underlie all good relationships and later bring about satisfying and safe sexual activities.

• Homosexuality •

The medical and psychological professions consider homosexuality an adult condition rather than an adolescent one, yet homosexuality is a major topic of conversation among adolescents. Teenagers are dramatically aware of the physical and emotional sexual changes happening in their own bodies and almost all, at some time, feel concern about their sexual identity because their own feelings and development seem out of step with those of their peers.

Being different is difficult at any age and particularly so when you're going through puberty. A person's *understanding* of his sexual identity develops over a long period of time. Despite the publicity given early adolescent heterosexual activity, many grow into it very slowly. Their entire adolescent years may be a time of quiet growth and strong personal interests that involve little sexual activity of any kind.

Children enter their middle-school years with nearly all of their friends and activities taking place with members of their own sex. If this stage lasts long and is focused on one particular friend sometimes a parent complains, "Why does Sally have to spend the night here again? You see each other every day of the week. What's with the two of you?" These are scary words to a large, muscular athlete who may already be wondering why she doesn't enjoy the school dances, isn't being pursued by boys, and isn't sure she wants to be.

There's a vast amount of public thought and media coverage now being given to the sexual, political, legal, and social rights of adults singularly attracted to those of their own sex. Our children hear a lot about homosexuality, but they don't know very much about it. Neither do we adults.

While most people develop in a heterosexual direction, no one knows why a relatively few others develop an exclusively homosexual orientation. We do know that homosexuality is not an illness, nor a condition that happens because of an ineffective parenting style or an imbalance of sexual hormones. However, a growing body of recent evidence indicates that homosexuality has a major genetic component, one that influences the sexual orientation of a significant number of those people who are homosexual.

It is becoming increasingly accepted that homosexuality is not the result of individuals making a conscious choice to become homosexual. They just are and we don't yet have firm answers as to why.

In light of this thinking, parents who have concerns about an adolescent's sexuality will do well to recognize there is nothing they can or should do to influence their adolescent's sexual orientation. Indicating concern about a child's involvement with another of the same sex can lead to a young person's premature and wrong labeling of himself about his sexual preference.

The term homosexual is best used to refer to an adult who is exclusively sexually attracted to people of his/her own sex and seeks sexual intimacy and relationships with them

Most children in the process of growing up have some homosexual thoughts, desires, and emotional experiences. Letting discussions on these thoughts and ideas be an acceptable topic of conversation in your home will help your children recognize that such feelings and experiences do not determine their sexual identity. If, as they grow older, their sexual orientation is homosexual, your earlier open attitude will have allowed them valuable time for their growth.

Choosing to discuss diversity in sexual preference isn't easy for most parents. Adult beliefs and anxieties about homosexual activities leave some parents in the same difficult position as when talking about early adolescents becoming heterosexually active. We know all the problems that can arise and we don't want those for our children. If we talk about homosexuality, aren't we also acknowledging that our child might be, or become, homosexual? Yes, and it does happen.

Some children become adult homosexuals and openly acknowledge their orientation. Others deal with the fear, limitations, and prejudice that surround their sexual orientation by living a life of secrecy. As parents, our communication with an adolescent who doesn't follow the sexual growth patterns of his peers can either be shaped by the judgmental attitudes we've had passed on to us by others, or we can reject prejudice and put our efforts into positive actions that demonstrate acceptance and love, that honor individuality and build healthy family relationships.

• The Value of Family Interaction •

We know effective parents take time to do a lot of talking with their children. They talk about thoughts, feelings, and situations; they consider goals, problems, and solutions. They examine all kinds of behavior, discuss choices, and consider consequences. Children reared in such a growth climate learn through practice to think about what they're going to do before they do it.

These children also develop a strong sense of their own value as they and their parents discuss repeatedly the important issues in their lives. All through this book, we've been talking about the skills and techniques that encourage good communication and problem solving. Using these same skills on matters that pertain to our children's sexuality is particularly worth the effort.

A strong sense of her own worth is perhaps a child's best protection against unplanned, unsafe, unwanted, indiscriminate, or premature sexual behavior.

Understanding
Teen Sexuality

• Steps to Change •

Consider your child's position. Daily your child's thoughts are influenced by a cultural climate that promotes a "live now, grow up fast" sexual philosophy. Yet, teens want and need parent input.

Accept your position. You cannot change the world or control your child's behavior. However, the standards you hold, the values you live by, and the talking you and your child do can make a difference.

Commit to discussing specifically all sexual issues with your child. Use topics from sex education classes and the mature sexual environment in which she lives. Begin during the preteen years.

Seek your teen's viewpoint. Focus on his opinions, concerns, and feelings. Resist arguing. Discuss choices. Give accurate information.

Give special attention to the subject of sexual safety. Use topics from magazines and news reports. Discuss prevention, escape, and the reporting of abusive behavior from strangers or acquaintances.

Recognize we're all vulnerable when it comes to our child's developing sexuality. Seek professional counseling if you need help in this area.

11

Parental Persistence

New Belief: *Problems will be with us always and our ability to handle them will always be less than perfect.*

• Moving Beyond the Past •

Parents must accept not only their children's unsteady growth, but their own. While solving problems is the business of life in its ever-changing aspects, our wisdom in doing so is limited daily by our knowledge and circumstances. Again and again, we're forced to face the reality of our imperfect parenting abilities.

You may be worrying about the critical things you've missed or mishandled at your house. Your child may be in middle school and already be having serious problems. You may sense the groundwork hasn't been laid for the growth you both need and your mind is full of fear and regret. You may not know how to begin.

First, you'd never think of taking credit for all your child's successes in life, so don't waste time blaming yourself or earlier circumstances for your child's growing-up difficulties. Blaming yourself, or your child, for past behavior and seeing it as a long-term handicap cripples you both.

You can't truly free your child from blame and guilt until you free yourself.

Given our circumstances in life, most of us generally do the best we can with what we have, know, and understand. You may recall my saying earlier that children learn to make good decisions by first making poor ones. In the same way, we learn to be better parents.

The problems that cause our pain and frustrations also challenge us to grow. Recognizing behavior you regret and acknowledging it to yourself, and to the other person when appropriate, starts the process of change. Your reading of this book has given you new information and tools. Maybe you've taken some of the first steps suggested, and while there's improvement, you and your child are still having problems. Yes, because problems are the way of life.

• The Complex Nature of Parenthood •

Letting our children see us struggle with the troublesome nature of parenthood isn't necessarily bad. Few things are as simple as we try to make them.

We live with conflicting truths and working through the reality of each problem is an ongoing part of being a parent. Children need freedom and they need rules. Children need praise and they need correction. Individual needs must be honored and the needs of others must sometimes take precedence.

• Truth and Trust, But at What Cost? •

Our mature and challenging 14-year-old Ginny had our tentative permission to attend a surprise birthday party for a male school friend. When I asked for the parent's telephone number the night of the party so I could call to check that they'd be there, she replied, "Don't bother, they won't."

Of course, thoughts of alcohol, drugs, and sex flashed through my mind. I knew all about "partying." "Then whatever made you think I'd let you go?" I asked, astonished.

"Because I told you the truth! I could have lied, said we were going to a movie, and then gone to the party instead. You'd never have known."

She was right. She was the youngest in her crowd. Many of her friends had their driver's licenses. Circumventing us would be easy, and she and I both knew her truthfulness was a big issue. Resentfully, I acknowledged her power, and spent the next few minutes trying to talk to her about the problems she might meet in an unsupervised party, and how she might best deal with them.

Leaving her room, I silently asked God to keep her safe and to handle what I obviously couldn't. Still, I felt terrible. I banged around in the kitchen, on edge with everyone. Suddenly, I realized that our daughter, after talking several times on the telephone, had settled in the den in her pajamas. Casually she explained, "No one could get a car and Sue forgot to make the cake. We're not going."

Thank you, God, for a second chance! I now knew that if the price I must pay for her truth was my automatic permission, then the cost was too high. I shared this with Ginny and commented on the investment we both had in her growth, but also in making our relationship work. While truth was a part of it, it wasn't the only part.

"As the parent of a 14-year-old there are still times when I'll need to use my judgment and refuse the permission you want. These times will lessen, but tonight I should have said 'no.' I don't want you to lie, but if you do, then that is a choice you make. I want our relationship to be built on trust, but I can't give up being a parent to get the truth from you."

As you see, our growth is as important as our children's. I was getting practice in looking at a bigger picture, at my responsibility for my behavior and her for hers, in our movement toward her adulthood.

• Resistance to Rules •

Let's take curfews, for example. They seem simple in principle. A parent considers the child's age and experience and then decides the reasonable time for his return home from an outing. This works fine when we are the major source of transportation, know our youngsters' friends and their parents, and are generally involved in their activities.

Unfortunately, as soon as our services are no longer needed, we're at the mercy of our child's desires and view of what a curfew means. To most children, the lack of one is a major sign of adulthood. Therefore, the earlier the curfew, the more his parents doubt his maturity; no matter how late the time, it's never late enough. Due to its restrictive nature, a curfew is a challenge to adolescents.

What better way for teenagers to feel their own power than by not coming home when we say they must? They may listen to our lectures, experience our displeasure, and submit to our discipline, yet they know we cannot *make* them abide by the curfew. *Curfews are not a solution; they're an opportunity for learning.*

• How Long Should We Struggle? •

When Ginny was a junior in high school, meeting curfew began to be a problem. In the beginning, there were excuses and apologies, then arguments and resentment. Finally, in her senior year, she returned home later and later. Rational and irrational talks, upset parents, and logical consequences did not get the desired results.

After one particularly upsetting weekend, and with no friendly tones left, I suggested we each write down our feelings about the situation and how the other's behavior affected us. We then exchanged papers. She hated knowing she'd get an argument from me anytime she called to tell me she was running late, hated having an exact time to be in, and hated my meeting her at the door, angry and full of lectures when she was late.

Words in my defense clamored to come out, but then I realized I'd said it all on the page: "I know before you leave you haven't really accepted our need for you to be home at a certain time, so I start being angry as soon as you walk out the door. Then I never know how late you'll be, so I'm upset about that, for your not calling home, for arguing with me when you do, and for all the bad feelings between us."

My last words caught her attention. "Yeah, having you so mad, that's the worst part for me."

My anger receded a little. "I know you want more independence, but can't we find something that will work for both of us?"

"I don't know, Mom. If I'm ten minutes late I know you'll be waiting up and already angry. If I've had anything to drink I have to listen to a lecture and see you get madder and madder as you talk. I hate it, I go to bed feeling terrible, with all the good memories of the evening gone. I guess I dread coming home, so I don't think about the time. Soon, I'm past curfew and I smell like beer, so what does it matter? You're going to be mad anyway."

"So what do you want me to do? Act like it's not happening, and that it's okay for you to disregard state laws and our rules? Pretend I like it? Is that your answer?"

I stopped. I could feel my voice rising. I couldn't even attempt to paraphrase her words or understand her feelings. My body tightened as I struggled for control.

"Mom, you don't like it and I know it. I don't get an allowance because I use it to buy cigarettes and beer. I can't use the car at night because sometimes we 'party' and I come home late." Her voice became thoughtful. "I know you won't go to bed until I'm home, but maybe I'd try harder if you weren't so upset when I do get here. It seems like all we do is argue."

Then it hit me. All my anger, tension, and inability to communicate couldn't be just about her curfew. Neither could the drinking be the whole problem. While Clif and I hated the partying her group did, we knew we couldn't control her behavior once she was out of our sight. Still, there had to be more to my reaction.

"All right," I said. "Let's take a break for thinking and meet again later."

• Understanding and Dealing with Hidden Fear •

Obviously part of my anger with this daughter came from feeling victimized by her behavior. She was deciding the time she'd come home, not us, and that wasn't right. But why wasn't it? She was 17, and her next oldest sister went to college at that age. Why was this child's curfew so important to me?

Then I felt the fear rising in my throat: Fear for her safety, health, and future. Fear that if she didn't obey our curfew, we'd have lost all control. Devastating fear covered by anger.

When Ginny entered high school, she'd announced, jokingly we thought, that she wouldn't be following in her older sisters' footsteps. What she meant was, "Popularity and fun are going to be more important to me than grades."

Immediately, she proved the seriousness of her statement by seeking a group that shared her goals. Since then, hardly a semester had passed without a crisis of some kind as a result of her precocious, challenging behavior.

Now, I moved deeper and realized, with the pain such awareness brings, that alcoholism and drug addiction were a possibility for Ginny. She'd begun an active social life of dating and parties much earlier than our other children and she did use alcohol irresponsibly.

Yet, so did some of our older children, our friends, even ourselves in our earlier days. Alcoholism was a possibility for anyone. So were all those other things I feared: car accidents, rape, unplanned pregnancies, illnesses, and sexually transmitted diseases. They didn't happen just to teenagers.

Yet, here I was, believing that if we could get her obedience to a curfew we'd also get her sobriety, safety, and morality. My belief was unrealistic. No wonder I met her in anger.

When Ginny and I met again, I was honest and explicit about the fears I'd found beneath my anger and the belief I'd held that her coming home on time would prevent terrible things from happening to her.

"There are endless things that can arise in life to threaten your well-being and you're the one who must handle them as they occur. They can happen when you're drinking and when you're not drinking, when you're obeying laws and when you're not. You need the freedom to be alert to every situation and consider for yourself what is safe and best for you to do.

"Hereafter we'll talk about your plans for the evening and you'll give us the approximate time you expect to be home. I may stay up or I may not, it isn't important. You focus on your safety and I'll focus on . . . on . . ." Suddenly I smiled, "On our relationship!"

That night when she came in a little later than her chosen time, I put my arms around her, gave her a real hug, and said, "You're home safe. You've taken care of yourself and that's the important thing." For the first time in months, she returned my hug in a genuine manner.

• Don't Ever Give Up on Your Child! •

Let's say you have a youngster who acts out constantly. You know the youngster I mean. The one who is caught in a pattern of unhealthy action: irritating, unsafe, rule-flaunting, illegal, or immoral. She ignores home responsibilities, cuts school, talks back, runs with the wrong crowd, and has been found shoplifting. He

goes into yelling tantrums with you and his siblings over everything, hangs out at the local park when he's supposed to be home,
abuses car privileges, and smokes marijuana.

You've been reading this book and trying to move away from
judgment, power, and punishment, but you're totally discouraged. Your efforts to communicate and problem solve positively
seem to help a little, and then another crisis happens.

Your attempts to respond without overreaction are taken as
sarcasm, and within moments, you've lost your temper. The war
is on again and by the time the battle ends, you're only a step
away from saying, "Get out. Go. Do what you want to do. You
live your life and I'll live mine. I give up!"

Don't give up! Not now. Not ever.

Most youngsters, in their struggle toward maturity, at some time
develop prolonged problem behaviors that cause us *great* distress. A
farmer, father of a large number of successful children, was once
asked if he had a favorite among his many offspring. He thought for
a moment and then replied, "No, not a favorite, but there was always one, at any given time, I'd gladly swap for a horse."

If you're looking for a man with a horse to swap, stay with me
while I share some of the things that have encouraged Clif and me
to persist.

*Believe in your ability, and your youngster's, to grow through
these problems and to forgive and forget.* A parent-child relationship that has been present since the child's birth or from an early
age can never really end. Even if you literally disown your son or
daughter, the anger and separation will affect you both the rest of
your lives. Believe in commitment and deliberately recommit to
your relationship.

Recommitment is a necessary step in any long-term, worthwhile undertaking. Begin by not making the quality of your relationship dependent upon your child's changing behavior.
Acknowledge your fears and your recommitment. Then, stay on
the job as a loving parent.

Give up the response of anger. Remember that beneath anger
there are other feelings at work. They are often hidden, but sometimes not. You may even believe that your child will not change
unless you express your pain and fears in angry behavior and
words. This is an untrue belief. *No one* responds well to anger.

If anger and resentment have become a regular pattern of response for you, and changing your response is difficult, seek counseling for yourself. If your child is having major problems in two or more areas of his life (school, home, social) or intense anger is his immediate response to most situations, find a counselor for yourself who specializes in adolescent difficulties and encourage your child's participation.

Remember, as you make effective changes in your behavior and attitude, and stay firm in your commitment to those changes, your child *will* change his responses. You're creating an environment that invites change.

Dare to take action where you can be effective. List the things that keep you awake nights, haunt your days, and create problems with your child. Decide who owns the problems and what your course of action will be. Evaluate regularly how you're doing on taking care of the problems or parts of problems that belong to you.

You are not giving up if you insist on temporary relief. Recognize that you do not have the power or the responsibility to resolve your teenager's problems, and *right now* you may not be able to handle any more of his lying, stealing, drug use, or whatever it is that's threatening your home and peace of mind.

You are not giving up if you talk with your teenager about staying temporarily with a friend or relative while you both consider what has been happening and what you each are willing to do to improve the situation.

You are not giving up if you insist on professional counseling for all concerned, prior to and following his return. Indicate your desire to see the situation improve for *everyone*.

Accept the possible reality of your worst fears. Life's difficulties happen to most of us, in some way, at some time. When they do, we either choose to grow through them or we cope by making unproductive choices that benefit neither us nor our world.

Choose to grow. Take care of yourself. Exercise and eat well. Seek counseling and ongoing support groups. Read educational and inspirational books and magazines.

Move through fear to hope. Fear binds us to what is happening now and transports our worry to the future. Hope makes us think about love, growth, and miracles. Fear takes away options; hope encourages change. Fear weakens will power; hope empowers actions. With hope, we know there is always another day, another year. Hope is the foundation upon which persistence rests.

Discouragement is contagious, but so is optimism. Encourage yourself with self-talk:

- I participate in my child's growth, but I'm not in charge of it.
- Inwardly my child is becoming more than I can presently see.
- She doesn't have to agree with me today to change later.
- A judgmental comment invites a rebuttal.
- Relationships are more important than problems.

Have faith. When the unpaved mountain road your child chooses is rocky and full of pitfalls and dangerous curves, believe in the power of love, family, and growth. Faith is unquestionable and unquestioning belief. It anticipates, it expects, it precedes accomplishment. It's faith that gives us the ability to believe that a power within us, our children, and the road itself will help us all to navigate.

Vow to persist. For a month one summer, I regularly ate lunch with the kindest, wisest male counselor I have ever known and two of the most respected and competent men in our school district. It gave me great comfort to hear these mature, effective men reminiscing about their own unbelievably insensitive and unwise adolescent and early adult behavior.

Persistence means remembering our own growth and the many things we did that our parents didn't know about and would have "died over" if they had. Persistence means having faith that our children, too, will grow beyond their current behavior.

To persist is to continue despite obstacles; to carry on; to refuse to give up. We persist when we:

- Consistently take care of those parts of problems we own.
- Seek solutions cooperatively to those problems we don't own.
- Look for growth rather than behavior change.
- Focus on life-threatening dangers rather than social and status-oriented values.
- Know we have neither the right nor the power to decide the paths our maturing children will take for their learning.
- Practice love that *feels* like love.

• Recognizing and Managing Discouragement •

In a speech regarding delinquent youngsters and their emotional needs, Dr. Rudolf Dreikurs, the famous child psychiatrist and author of such books as *Children: The Challenge* and *The Challenge of Parenthood*, said he'd never known a child who was regularly failing to do what duty or law required, who was not *also* deeply discouraged.

Clif and I took these words to heart. We might not be able to change a child's behavior, but surely we could do something about her discouragement. Webster's dictionary says to discourage is to "make less confident or hopeful, to dishearten." Unfortunately, most of our communication with difficult children is about their deficiencies, which is very discouraging to both child and parent.

To encourage, then, must mean to make one *more* hopeful, confident, and cheerful. However, to be able to give those feelings, we have to be hopeful, confident, and cheerful ourselves.

———

It helped me to return again to those wonderful words by the philosopher Marcus Aurelius:

If you are distressed by something external, the pain is not due to the thing itself, but to your own estimate of it. This you have the power to revoke at any minute.

———

Our oldest daughter Della was coming for her first visit home since entering college. We'd had a difficult couple of years and I was determined to change my behavior and my discouraging ways with her.

For two days, surely I could refrain from all critical looks, strained expressions, and words of disagreement and advice. I knew that for too long I'd been focusing on her problems and that which was unhealthy in her behavior. I needed practice in being happy with this daughter, in using again those hopeful, light-hearted, "just-relating" phrases and touches that once had been such a part of our relationship.

She walked in the door and her immediate, enthusiastic comments about her good luck in getting the classes she wanted made it easy for me to suggest we relax over a cup of coffee. As she began to talk, suddenly my hand reached out and covered hers.

For several years, she'd had difficulties with her back and had been following recommended exercises and medical advice. Now, here she was, sitting crooked again, her upper body facing in my direction and her legs twisted to the side.

"Honey," I began, "you know when . . ." Instantly, she pulled her hand from mine and wariness covered her face. She'd caught in my words an old familiar tone and she was preparing herself for my "helpful, critical, good parent" comments.

Criticism is *never* encouraging. This time I recognized its damaging effect. I reached for her hand and started over. "I'm sorry, I shouldn't have interrupted. Tell me now about your classes. Your eyes were actually sparkling with your enthusiasm."

The weekend wasn't perfect, but it was better than others we had shared.

• Experiencing Encouragement •

It is encouraging to have one's personal uniqueness recognized positively.

Soon afterwards, Clif, who was still at home recovering from his illness, specifically requested my time of arrival from school. As often happened, I was late. His face was tight and his voice sarcastic as he asked, "So what happened today?"

What had happened was a difficult parent conference that ran too long, but I knew this wasn't a valid reason. My inability to leave school on time was a real problem to Clif and the children. They complained, I explained. Clif talked time management. I rationalized school emergencies and made promises. It was a continuing problem with no apparent solution.

So, I began a lie. "There was an accident on the freeway and traffic was all. . . ." Then, as I saw him struggle with his anger, I closed my eyes for a moment and shook my head.

I began again: "No, that's not true, and from your viewpoint, there's no good reason. I should not have given you a definite time if I didn't intend to honor it. My coming home is the focal point of your day, just as for years it was the other way around. How I'd have hated it if I'd never known when you'd be home."

Gently Clif put his arms around me and said, "Yes, but I can't change you, can I? Your intensity is part of you no matter what you're doing. It's there when you're preparing for company, planning an outing, or hunting for new furniture. I'd like you home at a regular time each day, but it's never going to be that way, is it? Not if you work the only way you know how."

• Defining Strengths •

In a few words, Clif's new understanding had moved my behavior from a weakness to a strength. If I am as I am when I work and play, why should I change what is possibly my strongest attribute?

Now I began to see our difficult daughter's behavior through the eyes of her future employers. I could almost hear their words: "Not argumentative, but goal directed; not difficult to please, but committed to excellence; not bossy, but knowledgeable; not self-centered, but self-motivated."

Had Clif and I been trying to change the unchangeable in our daughter? Despite our years of efforts to mold her ways to ones easier for our large family to cope with, she continued to fill her life and ours with extreme amounts of excitement, change, and challenge. She still tested limits, questioned those in authority, and sought new ways and beliefs—but did that mean her growth was wrong? Or just different?

In the weeks that followed, I found myself handling my work at school differently. I began by marking out certain afternoons when I would leave school on time and scheduling all parent conferences on those days before and during school hours. Paperwork tasks were for afterwards. Having my character traits validated as a strength rather than a deficiency apparently freed something within me. I wanted to make and honor the changes that would help my family.

With our daughter, I was now able to evaluate my comfort level of participation in her never-ending ideas and projects and remain there. At the same time, I could identify the underlying strengths she was developing and appreciate her need to use them in her life. Our arguments diminished and our communication improved.

The problems had not changed, but my attitude towards them had. For both our daughter and me, I wasn't trying to change weaknesses, I was managing strengths. What a difference!

• Finding Your Child's Strengths •

For a period of two days, decide to shift your attention from your child's negative behavior to building your relationship with him in a positive and encouraging manner.

Look beneath those irritating, outward expressions of your child's growing personality and find positive characteristics within or beneath them. When possible, identify by name the emerging adult strengths so that you can encourage your child honestly. Remember, you're working on your relationship, not your child's behavior.

———

Matt was in full adolescence, 6'4" tall, and still growing. He was awkward, uncooperative, and argumentative. We disagreed daily.

After a particularly bad morning, I decided I had to find something I liked in this child and use it to build our relationship in a more positive manner. He was right—most of our conversations with him were negative.

I called Clif from work and we agreed we'd give the strength treatment a chance. For two days we'd not flinch, correct, or criticize. Instead, we'd each commit ourselves to finding in Matt things we could like and then relate to him through them.

The book *Contact: The First Four Minutes,* written by Dr. Leonard Zunin and his wife Natalie Zunin, talks of how the first few minutes of each contact set the tone and direction of the conversation that will follow. I remembered their words that night as I opened the kitchen door and stepped into the house.

The instant Matt saw me, he began to move across the floor, doing a silly two-step, slip, slide, almost fall, slide again exit. He had a glass of milk in one hand and two bananas in the other. Prepared for disaster, I held my breath until he made it safely onto the carpet, then clapped my hands and exclaimed, "Do it again so I can watch your footwork."

As he did, I commented on his ability to catch himself each time at just the right place in the slips and slides, but couldn't figure out how he managed to keep the milk steady. His answer involved several minutes of talk and a slow-motion demonstration of the balance and coordination that went into his actions.

In another's efforts, we can always find a strength.

• Working on the Relationship •

At dinnertime, Clif and I made a point of listening to anything Matt said and responding with direct eye contact and the kind of intense, nonchallenging interest we'd have given an honored dinner guest. When a humorous comment made by Matt was lost in another child's interrupting words, Clif immediately went back to it. "What was that you said, Matt? My hearing aid didn't pick it up in the confusion."

Matt's remark had been so subtle, its full humor had really been missed by all of us. Now everyone roared. Then someone said, "The trouble is, Matt doesn't tell us when he's going to be funny." And that was funny. It also started Matt talking about sharing his dad's love of puns, and how playing around with them when he was little had led him to working with words and exaggerating situations until he'd found out what made people laugh.

Leaving the table that night, Clif squeezed my shoulder and grinned. Our dissatisfaction with this child was already changing into a more hopeful feeling.

The next morning, I ignored the four-letter words he used in a telephone conversation with his friend and decided to view the milk he'd left on the counter overnight as "just a happening." No one leaves milk out on purpose. Later, Clif noticed Matt's refusal to react to his younger sister's serious bait for a squabble, winked at him, and then whispered after she left the room, "Thanks, peacemaker."

It's always encouraging to have one's efforts—no matter how minor—recognized and appreciated.

———

That afternoon, Matt walked in with a serious face and the sad news that someone had stolen his new jacket from the sidelines while he was playing basketball. For the third time this month, his "carelessness" had caused a major problem.

In the past, all my words would have been negative and discouraging as I reviewed his lack of responsibility. Those words would have changed nothing. Now, it was easy to share his feelings and recognize his loss, then add, "Someone must have known how totally involved you get when you're doing something important and taken advantage of your concentration. I'm so sorry, Matt."

He stayed quiet for a bit, then he said, "Yeah, me too, but I should have known better than to have left the jacket there. You're right, I don't think of anything but the game when I'm playing." Then his head went up and he smiled. "Maybe that's why the coach says I'm a natural."

• Retrospective •

All through this book, you've seen Clif and me being challenged by the problems of our six children. You've seen us gain insights, change our attitudes, words, and behavior and then see our children change theirs. What you've not seen were immediate solutions that resolved all our family's difficulties.

Remember the word *judgment* written on the college professor's blackboard? That one simple word began a lifelong journey for us. Everything builds on something else. You've seen us learn about problem ownership, sharing power, and the recognition of strengths; about natural and logical consequences and the words and attitudes that weaken their effectiveness. You've also seen us handle one situation well and then do just what we vowed not to do on the next.

Yet, that's the way of change. All effective parents are ineffective parents at times. As problems are a part of life, so are the ups and downs that go with our imperfect skills at parenting our children.

We struggle, slip, and fall; then we take stock honestly and start over. We can do this because we're working with a process we trust: One that is dedicated to open communication and cooperative problem solving; to standards and values and individual growth. It's a process that leads with worthwhile steps to caring relationships and encouraging attitudes; to changing knowledge, new skills, and dramatic insights; to responsible, creative people.

The process is a parenting style with room built in for an ever-changing world, full of everyday human beings. Problems will still arise, but most will be resolved differently in accordance with our new learning. We'll recall a situation with a youngster in which we wondered how everything would work out, *but we didn't worry about it*. We'll smile as we remember the overreacting anger we avoided, the genuine listening we did, and the real problem solving that happened. We realize that the climate in our home is changing and we're experiencing on-the-job parent satisfaction!

——

All of the Tracy children are now on the other side of adolescence, and daily Clif and I are grateful for the capable, exciting young adults they've become, still close to us and each other. In our family, there is no generation gap. We share a common language—one you've seen us learning in every page of this book.

I wish the same positive outcome for you.

Parental Persistance

• Steps to Change •

Recognize the value of persistence. Persistence succeeds when all else fails. Accept problems as the everyday business of life. Don't ever give up on your child.

Recommit to the relationship and realistic expectations. When your child's choices are painful, recognize your limitations. Decide to reject the use of anger, threats, and character-rending statements as behavior-changing tools.

Take action where you can be effective. Work on the parts of a problem under your control. Seek your child's cooperation and responsibility on life-threatening dangers, rather than lesser issues.

Focus for forty-eight hours on improving relationships. Plan to use the first few minutes of any contact positively. Appreciate uniqueness. Do not frown, flinch, criticize, correct, or complain.

Practice encouragement. Create stress-free, short encounters with your teen. Appreciate the skills and effort your child applies to activities of his choice. Identify the positive behavior with the name of the adult strength it will eventually become.

Recommended Readings

• Articles •

"Authoritative Parenting and Adolescent Adjustment Across Varied Ecological Niches," Sanford M. Dornbusch, Ph.D. et al.[1] *Journal of Research on Adolescence*, 1 (1991):19–36.

"Current Patterns of Parental Authority," Diana Baumrind, Ph.D.[2] *Developmental Psychology*, 4 (1971):1–103. • Research on authoritarian, permissive, and authoritative parenting styles among preschool and elementary-school children.

"Effective Parenting During the Early Adolescent Transition," Diana Baumrind, Ph.D. *Advances in Family Research*, 2 (1991):111-163.

"A Linkage Between DNA Markers on the X Chromosome and Male Sexual Orientation," D. H. Hamer, S. Hu, V. L. Magnuson, N. Hu, A. M. L. Pattatucci. *Science*, Vol. 261, No. 5119 (July 16, 1993):321.

"Parental Styles and Adolescent Development," Diana Baumrind, Ph.D. *The Encyclopedia on Adolescence*, (1991):746-758.

"Patterns of Competence and Adjustment among Adolescents from Authoritative, Authoritarian, Indulgent, and Neglectful Families," Sanford M. Dornbusch, Ph.D. et al. *Child Development*, 62 (October 1991):1049–1065.

"The Relation of Parenting Style to Adolescent School Performance," Sanford M. Dornbusch, Ph.D. et al. *Child Development*, 58 (October 1987):1244–1257.

"Research News: Evidence for Homosexuality Gene." *Science*, Vol. 261, No. 5119 (July 16, 1993):291-292.

"Single Parents, Extended Households, and the Control of Adolescents," Sanford M. Dornbusch, Ph.D. et al. *Child Development*, 56 (April 1985):326–341.

"Teenage Sexual and Reproductive Behavior in the United States," Alan Guttmacher Institute, *Facts in Brief,* July 1991.

"Toward a Drug-free Generation: A Nation's Responsibility." *National Commission on Drug-Free Schools,* (September 1990):2–6.

"Trends in Behavioral Genetics: Eugenics Revisited," John Horgan. *Scientific American,* Vol. 268, No. 6 (June 1993):130-131.

[1]Members of the Stanford Center for the Study of Families, Children, and Youth, Stanford University, Stanford, California.

[2]Professor at the Institute for Human Development, University of California, Berkeley, California.

• Books •

Between Parent & Teenager, Haim G. Ginott, Ph.D. New York: Avon Books, 1971. • Effective dialogue and advice that illustrate better ways of communicating.

Confident Parenting, Mel Silberman, Ph.D. New York: Warner Books, Inc., 1988. • Creative ways of applying growth-producing skills.

Contact: The First Four Minutes, Leonard (Ph.D.) and Natalie Zunin. New York: Ballantine Books, 1988. • Concrete help for those having trouble with personal interactions.

Experts Advise Parents, Eileen Shiff, editor. New York: Dell Publishing, 1987. • Informative articles from 14 different authorities on the challenges and joys of child rearing. Reliable information, excellent resource suggestions.

Feel the Fear and Do It Anyway, Susan Jeffers, Ph.D. Florida: Harcourt Brace Jovanovich, 1987. • Easy to understand information on the causes of fear and how to work through them.

Growing Up Again: Parenting Ourselves, Parenting Our Children, Jean Illsley Clarke and Connie Dawson. San Francisco: Hazelden/ HarperCollins, 1989. • A most helpful book for parents who didn't receive effective parenting as they were growing up.

How to Deal with Your Acting-Up Teenager, Robert T. Bayard, Ph.D. and Jean Bayard, Ph.D. New York: Evans & Company, Inc., 1983. • Responsible, concrete advice on how to handle ongoing, tough adolescent situations.

How to Talk So Kids Will Listen & Listen So Kids Will Talk, by Adele Faber and Elaine Mazlish. New York: Avon Books, 1980. • Techniques and illustrations on communicating with children.

Liberated Parents, Liberated Children, Adele Faber and Elaine Mazlish. New York: Avon Books, 1975. • Easy to read, excellent book directed to parents of younger children, encouraging use of the style of parenting *Grounded for Life?!* presents.

Loving Your Child Is Not Enough, Nancy Samalin. New York: Penguin Books USA Inc., 1987. • While written for the parents of younger children, book's dialogues and suggestions are transferable.

No More Nagging, Nit-picking, & Nudging, Jim Wiltens. Sunnyvale, Calif.: Deer Crossing Press, 1991. • Full of specific advice on the parent behavior that builds an adolescent's self-esteem.

Parenting Teenagers: Systematic Training for Effective Parenting (STEP), Don Dinkmeyer and Gary D. Mckay. Minneapolis: American Guidance Service, Circle Pines, 1983. • Concise information in textbook form.

P.E.T.: Parent Effectiveness Training, Thomas Gordon, Ph.D. New York: Peter H. Wyden, Inc., 1970. • A classic on the handling of family problems through effective communication; see chapters 3 and 4.

Pick Up Your Socks . . . and other skills growing children need! Elizabeth Crary. Seattle: Parenting Press, Inc., 1990. • Absolutely crammed with good ideas and explanations on how to incorporate positive parenting into everyday family situations.

Psycho-Cybernetics, Maxwell Maltz, M.D. New York: Pocket Books, Div. of Simon & Schuster, Inc., 1960. • A wonderful, practical classic about our beliefs and how we form them.

Raising Self-Reliant Children in a Self-Indulgent World, H. Stephen Glenn and Jane Nelson, Ed.D. Rocklin, Calif.: Prima Publishing & Communications, 1989. • With their own terminology and dialogues, these authors offer structured steps for good growth in families.

Solo Parenting, Kathleen McCoy. New York: Signet, Div. of Penguin Books, 1988. • This book discusses the unique problems of single parenting in helpful ways.

The Teenage Body Book, Rev. ed., Kathy McCoy and Charles Wibbelsman. New York: Pocket Books, Div. of Simon & Schuster, Inc., 1984. • Comprehensive and helpful information for teenagers and parents.

Toughlove, Phyllis and David York, Ted Wachtel. New York: Bantam Books, 1983. • Offers real help to parents with ongoing, serious problems or crises.

When Good Kids Do Bad Things, Katherine Gordy Levine. New York: Pocket Books, Div. of Simon & Schuster, Inc., 1991. • Particularly good reading in chapters 8 and 9 where author addresses specifically the problems of teens rushing into serious, risky behavior.

You & Your Adolescent, Laurence Steinberg, Ph.D. & Ann Levine. New York: Harper Perennial, 1990. • A well-researched, all-encompassing manual for parents. Good, succinct advice about problems; list of resources.

Your Child's Self-Esteem, Dorothy Corkille Briggs. New York: Doubleday & Company, Inc., 1975. • A parenting classic that deals with love, self-esteem, and the discipline of children of all ages.

Index